COLLINS GEM
CATS

COLLINS GEM
Chinese
ASTROLOGY

COLLINS GEM
Classic
BOOKS

COLLINS GEM
Classic
FILMS

D1394624

COLLINS GEM
HORSES
& PONIES

QUEENS

GEM
MUSHROOMS
& TOADSTOOLS

COLLINS GEM
SNAKES

COLLINS GEM
SPIDERS

COLLINS GEM
STRESS
Survival Guide

COLLINS GEM
TAROT

COLLINS GEM
WINE
Guide

COLLINS GEM
WORLD
atlas

COLLINS GEM
YOGA

COLLINS GEM
ZODIAC
Types

SAINTS

Robin Blake

HarperCollins*Publishers*

The right of Robbie Blake to be identified as the author of this work has been asserted by him in accordance with the Copyright, Designs and Patents Act 1988

HarperCollins*Publishers*
Westerhill Road, Bishopbriggs, Glasgow G64 2QT

First published 2001

Reprint 10 9 8 7 6 5 4 3 2 1 0

© Essential Books 2001
All drawings © Barbara Saulini
All photographs reproduced by kind permission of the Art Archive

ISBN 0 00 710148-1

All rights reserved. Collins Gem® is a registered trademark of HarperCollins*Publishers* Limited

Printed in Italy by Amadeus S.p.A.

Contents

Introduction

Saints are the heroes and heroines of the Church – those deemed to have lived such good lives, or endured death so perfectly, as to be guaranteed an afterlife in Paradise. The cult of the saints arises because of their aura, the sense that they hold a golden key to the puzzle of existence. Having the ear of God, they also act as advocates, pleading for divine help on our behalf. In medieval times the saints were a popular passion. Akin to today's celebrities, they were continually emulated and discussed by their 'fans', while pilgrimages to their shrines were the forerunners of modern mass-tourism. Images and relics of saints were highly prized, while books of their lives were the first truly popular best-sellers.

This book aims to provide a worthwhile selection from the thousands of saints in the calendar. People in all walks of life are represented, from a Holy Roman Emperor (Henry II) to the peasant girl Maria Goretti, from Nicholas Owen, a carpenter who made priest holes, to the politician and power-broker Sir Thomas More; from Ugandan saint Joseph Mkasa to Maximilian Kolbe, a martyr of Auschwitz. There are clues in these lives to the causes for which each saint may be invoked, some obvious, others more obscure. Enquire within if you want to know why Clare is the patron of television and Jude a specialist in desperate causes.

How is a person raised to sainthood? In the early Church, canonisation did not exist. A saint simply emerged by popular acclaim, particularly if there were miracles around the tomb or relics. But eventually the Catholic Church began to handle matters more judiciously, with what was effectively a legal trial in which a postulator and a 'devil's advocate' were appointed to argue the case for and against a particular candidate. A three-stage process is followed today. First the candidate must be formally accepted as a 'Servus Dei' (Servant of God). This, after exhaustive investigation, is followed by beatification, in which the candidate is given the title 'Blessed'. The final stage, which may not be reached for decades, even centuries, brings full canonisation in Rome.

The official source for the lives of all saints in the Catholic Church is the *Acta Sanctorum,* while the most colourful (and unreliable) is Jacobus de Voragine's *The Golden Legend,* possibly the most widely read book in medieval Europe. This work is sometimes mentioned under 'Sources'. Some near-contemporary biographies have also been mentioned.

THE SAINTS

Aelred (Ethelred)

Abbot
1110–67

Aelred's father and grandfather were both priests of Hexham, Northumbria, at a time before clergy were invariably celibate. As a teenager he served King David I in Scotland and, by the age of 24, he was Edinburgh Castle's head steward. But, hearing that a group of eleven men had founded Britain's first Cistercian monastery in Yorkshire, Aelred returned to England to join them. Elected abbot in 1147, he made Rievaulx one of the most powerful monasteries in Britain, and the original eleven swelled to a community of 650. Aelred upheld its standards by exercising uncommon gentleness and good sense. He travelled and wrote widely, especially on the spiritual value of common friendship. He died at Rievaulx, in an outhouse next to the infirmary. The monastic ruins are among the most romantically situated in Britain.

Feast: 3 February
Shrine: Rievaulx Abbey, near Helmsley, North Yorkshire
Writings: sermons, prayers, letters and the books *On Spiritual Friendship* and *The Mirror of Charity*

Agatha

Virgin and Martyr
d. 3rd century. Canonised by early tradition

Few martyrs have been subjected to more graphically sexual tortures than Agatha. Born to wealthy Christian parents below Sicily's Mount Etna, she was a beautiful girl dedicated to virginity. After rejecting the amorous attentions of an official, Quintinian, she was confined in a brothel where her purity was miraculously preserved. In fury, Quintinian prosecuted her as a Christian and she was condemned to have her breasts torn away by pincers. These wounds were healed in a vision of **St Peter**, whereupon Agatha was dragged across burning coals until she died. These salacious details made her a favourite subject in art, often with her amputated breasts displayed on a plate. The similarity between these and loaves is said to have resulted in the blessing of bread on her feast day.

Feast: 5 February
Patron of bell foundries, nurses, Sicily, Malta
Causes: earthquakes, volcanic eruptions, fire, the protection of Sicily
Symbols in art: excised breasts on chafing dish, pincers, burning torch
Source: *The Golden Legend*

Agnes

Virgin and Martyr
d. *c.*304

Agnes was born in Rome during Emperor
Diocletian's persecution of Christians. As with
Agatha, she was a Christian girl who, at 12 or 13, refused to
yield her virginity to an important pagan suitor. She was
paraded nude through the streets to a brothel and, later, put
to death by being stabbed in the throat, appearing
afterwards to her parents with a lamb, symbol of youth and
purity. At the monastery of St Agnes in Rome lambs are
blessed each year, their wool dedicated to the weaving of
papal vestments. Agnes's cult grew after her death and she is
one of the earliest saints of her class to be venerated. Her
own foster sister St Emerentiana was stoned to death while
praying at Agnes's tomb.

Feast: 21 January
Patron of young girls, gardeners
Cause: charitable work
Shrines: a church raised above her tomb in the Via
   Nomentana, Rome, *c.*350; modern Rome has St Agnes-
   Without-the-Walls
Symbols in art: lamb, sword, palm
Source: *The Golden Legend*

*A 15th-century representation of St Agnes with the Lamb of Christ,
the symbol in art with which she is associated (Dagli Orti)*

Aidan

Abbot and Missionary
d. 651

An Irishman, Aidan was a monk of Iona sent to evangelise Northumbria. He founded the celebrated abbey at Lindisfarne, from where, with the support of the local Christian king, Oswald, he travelled much, preaching and performing miracles and spreading the Christian message in the Celtic, as distinct from the Roman, style. **Bede**, by whose time the Ionan Celtic forms were regarded as obsolete, nevertheless had high praise for Aidan's goodness, gentleness and moderation.

Feast: 31 August
Shrine: Lindisfarne
Symbols in art: stag, torch
Source: Bede's *History of England*

Alban

Martyr
d. *c*.209

Regarded as the earliest English martyr, Alban's dates are uncertain. He was a pagan Roman officer at Verulamium who, during an outbreak of anti-Christian persecution, sheltered a priest on the run and was converted by him. With the search party at the door, he changed clothes with the priest and was himself caught and beheaded. On the way to his death he is said to have parted the waters of the River Colne to enable a large crowd of onlookers to reach the execution place, Holmhurst Hill, which became the site of his shrine. It is now the cathedral of St Alban's.

Feast: 22 June (17 June C of E)
Shrines: St Alban's Cathedral, Hertfordshire; Angers, France
Source: Bede's *History of England*

Ambrose

Father of the Church
340–c.397

Ambrose was among the most influential Christians of his era, and is venerated as one of the four Fathers of the Church. A son of the praetorian prefect of Gaul, he grew up at Trèves, where a swarm of bees is said to have settled on his head without harm, but gifting him with honeyed eloquence. Educated in Rome in the years immediately following Emperor Constantine's momentous conversion to Christianity, he trained as a lawyer, entered government service, and became a highly successful governor of Liguria and Aemilia, based at its powerful capital, Milan. He was elected the city's bishop in 373 even before he had undergone baptism as a Christian, and went on to lend his great debating skills to the Catholic side in its damaging and violent dispute with the Arians. His success made him a key figure in the establishment of Orthodox Catholicism throughout Western Europe and, in paintings, he is sometimes shown handling a whip, with which to chase heretics and sinners from his church.

Feast: 7 December
Patron of Milan, bees, waxworkers
Shrine: Basilica of St Ambrose, Milan
Symbols in art: pen, three-lash whip, beehive, St Luke's ox, dove
Writings: *De Mysteriis, De Officiis Ministrorum, De Virginibus, De Fide, Commentary on St Luke.* Also hymns

Andrew

Apostle and Martyr
1st century

Andrew was the first of the Apostles – a fisherman from Bethsaida in Galilee who, as a follower of **John the Baptist**, witnessed Christ's baptism in the Jordan. Jesus called on Andrew to switch allegiance, which he did, simultaneously introducing his younger brother Simon **Peter** to Jesus. For a while they were part-time disciples but, when Jesus later returned to Galilee, they abandoned their fishing and were appointed 'fishers of men'. Andrew's later career is obscured by many legends, including one that he envangelised Scythia (Russia). The 3rd-century 'Acts of Andrew' are apocryphal. The story told of his death is that he converted the wife of the governor of Patras in the Peloponnese, persuading her to refuse sex to her husband. As a result, Andrew was arrested and crucified, bound by ropes to the famous X-shaped cross. In the Eastern Church he occupies a place almost as central as that of his brother in the West. His bones were allegedly brought to Scotland in the 4th century.

Feast: 30 November
Patron of Greece, Russia, Scotland, the Duchy of Burgundy, the Order of the Golden Fleece
Causes: gout, stiff-neck, sore throat
Shrines: St Andrews, Scotland; St Peter's, Rome
Symbols in art: saltire cross, fishes and fishing net, rope
Source: Mark 1: 16–18, John 1: 40–42

Anne

Mother of the Virgin Mary
1st century

Jesus's grandmother is unmentioned in the New Testament but her legend is told – with that of her wealthy husband, Joachim the Levite – in the apocryphal Book of James (2nd century). For 20 years the couple were stigmatised for their childlessness until an angel appeared to Joachim promising Anne a daughter, **Mary**. At home she had the same vision and ran joyfully to meet Joachim at the Golden Gate of Jerusalem 'and hung upon his neck'. This story is similar to the Old Testament account of Abraham and Sara, and the birth of Samuel to Hannah. Anne is bound up with the Immaculate Conception and, in art, most frequently appears in cycles of the life of the Virgin. Her sister, traditionally called Hismeria, was **John the Baptist**'s grandmother. In Brittany the cult of St Anne is thought to have continued that of pagan mother-goddess Nanna.

Feast: 26 July
Patron of Canada, housewives, cabinet-makers
Shrines: St Anne d'Auray, Brittany; St Anne's Church, Jerusalem; relics in Vienna, Cologne
Symbols in art: lily, holding the infant Mary
Source: *Protoevangelium of James*, *The Golden Legend*

Anselm

Bishop and Doctor of the Church
1033–1109. Doctor 1720

Anselm was at heart a theologian but his appointment as Archbishop of Canterbury forced him to be much involved in Church politics. Born at Aosta, Italy, he became a monk of Bec, in Normandy, at the late age of 27. His learning and wisdom led to his election to Canterbury in 1092, launching him into a decade of bitter disputes about the English Crown's powers over the Church. An accord was reached in 1103 and his remaining years were more tranquil. His writings centre on a desire to reconcile reason with faith and he has been called the Father of Scholasticism. He was a passionate early opponent of the slave trade.

> **Feast:** 21 April
> **Shrine:** Canterbury
> **Writings:** *Cur Deus Homo?* ('Why Did God Become Man?');
>   and many others
> **Source:** *Life of St Anselm* by Eadmer of Canterbury

Anthony of Padua (Ferdinand de Bulhoes)

Franciscan and Doctor of the Church
1195–1231. Canonised 1232; Doctor 1946

Anthony is the most celebrated Franciscan after **St Francis** himself. Already a priest, he joined the Order at the age of 25 and began a sensational career in Italy as a public preacher. Denouncing luxury among the clergy, and attacking doctrinal errors, he was

*St Anthony of Padua by El Greco (1541–1614)
in the Museo del Prado, Madrid (Dagli Orti)*

called the Hammer of the Heretics and, in a brief career of only nine years, soon established a reputation for sermons as powerful as they were learned. However, he was also known for gentleness and concern for social justice. Legend tells of an apparition of the Virgin and Child in his private cell. Anthony's tomb at Padua has always been a busy pilgrimage centre. He is credited with innumerable miracles and, except for the Virgin, is regarded as the most powerful of intercessors for anyone in distress.

Feast: 13 June
Patron of Padua, Portugal, the poor and oppressed, prisoners, travellers
Causes: things lost, shipwreck
Shrine: Basilica di San Antonio, Padua
Symbols: in art: lily, and kneeling to the Blessed Sacrament, book with child Jesus standing on it

Apollonia

Virgin and Martyr
d. 249

Among the female martyrs in the medieval lives of the saints, it is not only the young and pretty whose tortures are dwelt upon. Apollonia was an elderly deaconess in Alexandria who, during an outbreak of anti-Christian riots, was seized by the mob and, after refusing the ritual order that she sacrifice to pagan gods, had her teeth pulled out one by one. A bonfire was then lit and she was burned to death – or, as *The Golden Legend* reports, threw herself voluntarily into the flames. A considerable cult grew around her memory and she is often portrayed in art. However, the later West European artists tended to gloss over Apollonia's age and represent her as a beautiful young woman.

Feast: 9 February
Patron of dentists
Cause: dental disease
Symbols in art: forceps gripping a drawn tooth, gold tooth
Source: Letter of St Dionysus, Bishop of Alexandria

Augustine of Canterbury

Bishop and Missionary
d. 605

In the 6th century, the Celtic fringes of England were already Christian, but the southern heartlands remained pagan and in 596 **St Gregory the Great** sent a task force of 40 monks, led by the Roman monk Augustine, to convert the heathen provinces. They had immediate success in Kent, where the king, St Ethelbert, accepted baptism. For this reason, Augustine established his base – a church and a Benedictine monastery – at Canterbury, of which he became archbishop. Although a vigorous missionary, he could be tactless and high-handed. He argued long with the Celtic Christians to persuade them to harmonise with the reforms of the Pope in Rome, but they refused even to recognise him as their Primate.

Feast: 27 May (26 May in England)
Shrine: Canterbury
Symbols in art: well, baptising a king
Source: Bede's *History of England*

Augustine of Hippo

Father of the Church
354–430

One of the greatest figures of the early Church, Augustine is famous for having prayed, as a young man, 'make me chaste – but not yet!' He was born in what is now Algeria and brought up a Christian by his mother, St Monica. But as a student of philosophy at Carthage he lapsed, living riotously before taking a mistress who bore him a son, Adeotatus. In 384 Augustine moved to Milan as professor of rhetoric, where **St Ambrose** so impressed him that he was rebaptised in 387 by Ambrose himself. Augustine chose a monastic life at Hippo, in Egypt, but gained such a reputation as a preacher that in 396 he became the city's bishop, whereupon his fame began to spread around the Mediterranean. A compulsive writer and a theologian of genius, Augustine is the author of two classics of Christian literature and hundreds of other texts. His central idea of a political Church, in close alliance with the state, shaped Christianity for over a thousand years and his refinement of the doctrine of the Trinity is of vast historical significance. But he also had more

St Augustine of Hippo,
painted by
El Greco in 1590

St Barbara and the Disputation *by Simon Bening (1483/4–1561), from the collection of the British Library*

personal visions. Once on a beach he saw a child digging a hole in the sand. The child said he meant to empty the sea into that hole, which St Augustine said was impossible. 'Not more impossible,' the child told him, 'than for the finite mind to contain the infinite.' The child then vanished into the air.

Feast: 28 August
Patron of theologians, printers, brewers
Writings: *Confessions*, *The City of God*

Barbara

Virgin and Martyr
d. 303. Reduced to local status 1969

Born in Heliopolis on the Sea of Marmara, the beautiful Barbara is an entirely legendary figure. The story is that, as the object of her heathen father's obsessive jealousy, she was immured in a tower, spending her time in reading and meditation. Getting into correspondence with the theologian Origen, she became a Christian, which she inadvertently revealed to her father by having a third window added to the two already in her tower bathroom, to represent the light of the Trinity. In fury, the father had her tortured and then personally took her to a mountain top and beheaded her. On his way home he was struck by lightning and killed.

Feast: 4 December
Patron of Ferrara, Mantua, architects, builders, gunners, miners
Cause: danger from electrical storms and explosions
Symbols in art: bolt of lightning, tower, feather
Source: *The Golden Legend*

Barnabas

Apostle and Martyr
1st century

Like his friend **Paul**, Barnabas was styled an Apostle and may have personally known Christ, though he was not one of the original twelve. Born as Joseph, a Levite in Cyprus, he is first reported donating his property to the Christian community in Jerusalem and joining them in the aftermath of Christ's death. A relative of **St Mark**, he is credited with introducing Paul to **Peter** and the Jerusalem Christians. Barnabas was later entrusted with a mission to Antioch to establish a Christian group there, and took Paul with him. But the two men fell out over Barnabas's later insistence on collaborating with Mark, whom Paul distrusted and, after this, the two separated. Barnabas is the Apostle of Cyprus, where, by tradition, he was martyred at Salamis.

Feast: 11 June
Patron of Cyprus
Causes: hailstorms, peacekeeping
Symbol in art: book
Writings: The 'Epistle of Barnabas' is apocryphal
Source: Acts 9: 24, *The Golden Legend*

Bartholomew

Apostle and martyr
1st century

'Behold, an Israelite indeed in whom there is no guile' is how Jesus, in John's gospel, hails **Philip**'s friend Nathaniel, thought to be the same as the Apostle Bartholomew. He had already shown his directness on being assured by Philip that Jesus was the Messiah: 'Can there any good thing come out of Nazareth?' asked Nathaniel, a Canaanite. He is said to have specialised in casting out devils and has been variously associated with proselytising Lycaonia, Persia, Egypt, India and especially Armenia, where he was flayed and beheaded by King Astygas at Abanopolis on the west coast of the Caspian Sea.

Feast: 24 August
Patron of Armenia, plasterers
Symbols in art: flayed skin, knife
Source: (as Nathaniel) John 1: 45–51, *The Golden Legend*

*An illuminated manuscript of St Bartholomew
(c.1270) from the British Library*

Basil the Great

Doctor of the Church
330–79

Born at Caesarea in Cappadocia, Asia Minor, Basil was the first influential Christian teacher to sketch a theory of monasticism. But he was also powerful in preaching, public debate and concern for the wretched of the earth. He came from a wealthy and educated family, many of whom, including his mother, St Emmelia, experimented with living communally around a routine of work and prayer. Basil, after a brief secular career as a teacher of rhetoric, founded Asia Minor's first monastery and wrote its Rule – which is still the basis of life in all Orthodox monasteries. As his renown increased, Basil became Archbishop of Caesarea at a time when the Arian heresy, with its rejection of the Trinity, was gaining strength in Christendom. Standing in the front line of the debate, Basil's intervention was decisive in defeating Arianism in the Christian East. It also involved considerable personal bravery, as when he outfaced the Arian Emperor Valens. His episcopate was marked by investment in hospitals, almshouses and poor relief and he was an outspoken critic of clerical indiscipline and organised prostitution. As well as his mother, his father, Basil the Elder, his grandmother Macrina the Elder and his brother Gregory of Nyssa are all saints.

Feast: 2 January
Patron of Orthodox monks
Cause: monastic life
Symbols in art: book, dove, fire
Writings: ascetic writings ('Asceticon'); 'On the Holy
  Spirit'; 'Against Eunomius'

Bede the Venerable

Doctor of the Church
*c.*672–735. Doctor of the Church 1899

Bede was a man of Jarrow, in County Durham, who devoted
his entire life from the age of three to reading, writing and
the monastic life at the Abbey of St Peter. He wrote
biography, science, theology and history and is the only
Englishman recognised as a Doctor of the Church. Bede
scarcely ever left his monastery and yet contributed
enormously to our knowledge of the early English Church
and of his own times in general, making the so-called Dark
Ages considerably less dark. He was the first historian to
date events Anno Domini.

Feast: 27 May
Shrine: his tomb at Durham Cathedral
Writings: *History of England*

Benedict

Abbot and Founder of the Benedictine Order
*c.*480–547

Given the importance of monasticism in the Middle Ages, it is hard to understate the legacy of St Benedict. His pioneering Rule was one of the foundation stones for Western medieval civilisation, creating a pan European network of abbeys which were vital centres of learning and became transmitting-stations for ideas of every kind – theological, scientific, aesthetic and even culinary. Born at Nursia in Umbria, Benedict studied in Rome but hated city luxury and withdrew to a mountain hermitage. Soon disciples clustered around him and he organised them into a chain of monasteries. Benedict moved on in 529 to Monte Cassino, where he established a monastery. Here he died. His Rule, whose watchword was *laborare est orare* – to work is to pray – was never harsh but always practical. Benedict was devoted to his twin sister, St Scholastica.

Feast: 21 March
Patron of Catholic monks, cavers
Causes: Western monasticism, against thieving servants, poison and witchcraft
Shrine: Monte Cassino, Italy
Symbols in art: raven, broken cup
Writings: *The Rule of St Benedict*

Benedict and His Monks, *a fresco by Sodoma (1477–1549) in the abbey of Monteoliveto Maggiore in Siena (Dagli Orti)*

Bernadette (Marie Bernarde Soubirous)

Mystic
1844–79. Canonised 1933

Bernadette, one of the most celebrated saints of modern times, was the illiterate and asthmatic daughter of an impoverished miller in the small town of Lourdes, close to the French Pyrenees. On 11 February 1858, aged 14, she was gathering firewood beside the River Gave when she saw a vision of the Virgin, standing in the mouth of a cave on the opposite bank. The next day the vision reappeared, as it did on 16 further occasions. The last appearance came on 16 July. While pilgrims flocked to the site and miracle cures began to be reported, a sceptical Church tried to discredit Bernadette. She remained self-possessed, gently insisting on what the Virgin had told her – exhortations about world peace and the establishment of a pilgrimage centre at the grotto. While Bernadette withdrew into a convent at Nevers, the second of these wishes came true and Lourdes is now the greatest Christian pilgrimage centre, especially for the sick and dying.

Feast: 16 April
Cause: mortal and chronic sickness
Shrines: Lourdes, France, St Gildard's convent, Nevers, France

Bernard of Clairvaux

Abbot and Doctor of the Church
1090–1153. Canonised 1174. Doctor of the Church 1830

Bernard's driving personality galvanised the Cistercian Order, and the whole Church of his day. The son of a nobleman, he was born near Dijon. Aged 22 he joined the experimental monastery at Cîteaux, the first Cistercian house, after persuading four of his brothers and 27 friends to go with him. This is typical of Bernard's bullish leadership, though it seems a paradox that an extrovert should be so attracted to the strictest interpretation of the Benedictine Rule so far seen. After only three years at Cîteaux he founded a new house at Clairvaux in Champagne, which soon sprouted 68 dependent foundations, including **St Aelred**'s Rievaulx. But no monastery could contain Bernard and he became a pan-European power-broker between Popes and monarchs. In 1146, perhaps the most astonishing achievement of his long life was to launch the Second Crusade virtually single-handed, though since it was a miserable failure, this somewhat damaged his prestige. Bernard wrote well, founding a distinctive mystical spirituality on devotion to the Virgin. His cult never achieved the mass appeal of a **St Francis** or a **St Anthony**, though among educated Christians he was known as 'the honey-tongued doctor'.

St Bernard of Clairvaux (Dagli Orti)

Feast: 20 August
Patron of Cistercian monks
Shrine: Clairvaux, France
Symbols in art: beehive, mountain dog
Writings: *De Diligendo Deo* ('Of the Caring God');
De Consideratione ('Of Consideration')

Blaise

Bishop and Martyr
d. *c*.316

Very little is known about Blaise, though he
became the centre of a vigorous cult. He was
apparently a medical doctor elected bishop of
Sebastea in Armenia and executed by Governor Agricolaus
during the persecution of Christians in the reign of the
Eastern Emperor Licinius. Reputedly Blaise took refuge in
a remote hermit's cave, where wild animals came to him for
healing. Found by hunters, he was taken to Agricolaus and
after refusing to sacrifice to the pagan gods and suffering
various torments – such as having his body raked by the
sharpened teeth of a comb-like instrument – he was
beheaded. Before Blaise's trial, a child choking on a
fishbone was brought to him. He miraculously dissolved
the bone and the next day his mother smuggled in two
candles to light Blaise's prison. This is the origin of the

ritual carried out on his feast day, when throats are blessed
over a pair of crossed candles.

Feast: 3 February
Patron of Paraguay
Causes: afflictions of the throat, diseased animals
Symbols in art: comb, crossed candles
Source: *The Golden Legend*

Bonaventure (Giovanni di Fidanza)

Doctor of the Church
1221–74. Canonised 1482

Born at Bagnorea, Italy, he is said to have been nicknamed
Bonaventure by **St Francis** himself, who had cured him of a
childhood illness. He became a deeply learned friar who
earned his doctorate at Paris with his contemporary **Thomas
Aquinas**. Bonaventure was a leading defender of the
Franciscan Order against academic attacks, and was a
reforming minister general of the Friars Minor. His powerful
mind was put to work by the Pope, who had him draw up the
agenda for the Council of Lyons, a (temporarily) successful
attempt to heal Christendom's East–West schism. During
this Council Bonaventure died.

*St Bonaventure by Paolo Morando in the
Castellvecchio, Verona (Dagli Orti)*

Feast: 15 July
Patron of the Canary Islands
Symbol in art: cardinal's hat
Writings: *Of the Poverty of Christ, The Life of St Francis, Journey of the Soul to God*

Boniface

Bishop and Martyr
c.680–754. Canonised by tradition in Germany but not transferred to the universal calendar until 1874

Famed as the 'Apostle of Germany', Boniface was an Englishman. Born in Devon, he studied at Winchester and lived quietly until the age of 40 as a monk near Southampton. He then joined **St Willibrord** in the mission to Friesland, before moving on his own into Germany. By now a bishop, Boniface won many converts by defiantly cutting down the pagan Oak of Thor at Geismar in 722. He became a bishop and, in 747, Primate of Germany. This tireless organiser and traveller established sees and abbeys across Germany, including the great monastery at Fulda in 735. In his mid-70s he heard the Frieslanders had lapsed from Christianity after Willibrord's death and, resigning his office, set out to reconvert them. He was attacked and murdered by a gang of thugs at Dokkum, with a group of his followers.

Feast: 5 June
Patron of Germany, brewers, tailors
Shrine: Fulda Cathedral, Germany
Symbols in art: cauldron, club

Brendan the Navigator

Abbot
*c.*484–578

One of Ireland's most celebrated early saints,
Brendan came from Tralee, in County Kerry, and
was educated at St Jarlath's school at Tuam. He became a
great founder of monasteries, notably that at Clonfert,
Galway, where in his time more than three thousand monks
were trained for overseas missions. Brendan and his
questing monks sailed in leather boats to the offshore islands
in the west of Ireland and then – according to legend –
much further afield, even on an epic seven-year mission as
far as North America, which he called the Land of Promise.
The feasibility of this journey – using directions in the
phenomenally popular 10th-century *Navigatio Sancti
Brendani Abbatis* – was demonstrated in 1977 by the
adventurer Tim Severin, who sailed in a hide-covered boat
from Ireland to Newfoundland. But whether or not
Brendan really went to America, Irish monks inspired by
him reached not only the Western Isles of Scotland, but

Orkney, Shetland, the Faroes, Iceland, Greenland and the Canary Islands.

Feast: 16 May
Patron of sailors
Shrine: Mount Brandon, County Kerry
Symbols in art: a fish in hand, a burning candle or house
Source: *The Life of St Brendan the Navigator*

Bridget

Mystic and Foundress
1303–73. Canonised 1391

A Swedish noble, she was a mother of eight and a lady-in-waiting at the court of King Magnus II. After her husband's death in 1344 she spent four years as a contemplative, experiencing a series of visions and going on to found the Order of the Holy Saviour – Bridgettines – which was based at Vadstena but spread beyond Sweden. Bridget intervened in the Pope's handling of various political and theological issues and pressed unceasingly for the Papacy, then established at Avignon, to return to Rome, where she was by then living. In old age she set off disastrously for the Holy Land with her son Charles. On the way he had a scandalous affair with Queen Joanna of Naples and then died of fever. Returning directly to Rome, Bridget died soon afterwards. She is said to have mortified her flesh once with hot wax. Her fourth child, Catherine, continued her Bridgettine work and was herself canonised in 1484.

Feast: 8 October
Patron of Sweden, pilgrims
Cause: scholarship
Shrines: Vadstena, Sweden; San Lorenzo in Panisperna, Rome
Symbols in art: candle, flames, crown, cross, veil, dove, corn
Writings: *The Revelations of St Bridget*

Bruno

Founder of the Carthusian Order
1030–1101

A native of Cologne, he was educated at Rheims, where he later taught theology. In 1080 he refused the archbishopric of the city and resolved to be a hermit, moving in 1084 to La Grande Chartreuse in the remote French Alps. Here he formed a community which combined the severities of the hermit's life with the advantages of a Benedictine's. This formula, with each monk living in his own cell-hermitage, while coming together to pray and sing the office, proved very popular and brought Bruno fame. In 1090 he was

A wooden sculpture of St Bruno made in 1611 by Gregorio Fernández (c.1576–1636) (Dagli Orti)

ordered to Rome to advise his ex-pupil Pope Urban II. He left the city as soon as he could, founding a new charterhouse at La Torre, in Calabria, where he stayed until he died.

> **Feast:** 6 October
> **Patron of** the Carthusian Order
> **Shrines:** La Grande Chartreuse, France; La Torre, Italy
> **Symbols in art:** death's head, bishop's regalia underfoot, white Carthusian robe, star on his chest
> **Writings:** commentaries on the Psalms and St Paul

Catherine of Alexandria

Virgin and Martyr
d. c.310. Canonised 1623

Although she was one of the most popular saints of the Dark and Middle Ages, little is known about Catherine. A Christian noblewoman of Alexandria, she angered Emperor Maxentius by converting fifty of his philosophers whom the emperor then had burned to death. He imprisoned Catherine after she spurned his offer of marriage, telling him she was Christ's mystic bride. She then converted over two hundred of the royal entourage including the empress. They too were executed and Catherine sentenced to be broken on a spiked wheel – the 'Catherine Wheel' of fireworks. In fact, Maxentius's wheel broke and he had to have her beheaded.

St Catherine of Alexandria by Raphael (1483–1520) in the National Gallery, London (Eileen Tweedy)

St Catherine of Siena with Lily and Book
by Alessandro Franchi (Dagli Orti)

Feast: 25 November
Patron of Venice, Goa, philosophers, virgins, preachers, students
Causes: education, diseases of the tongue, eloquence
Shrine: Mount Sinai monastery, Egypt
Symbols in art: broken wheel, martyr's palm, wedding ring, dove
Source: *The Golden Legend*

Catherine of Siena (Catherine Benincasa)

**Mystic and Doctor of the Church
1347–80. Canonised 1461. Doctor of the
Church 1970**

The youngest of the 25 children of a Sienese
dyer, Catherine's austerity and mysticism gave her immense
authority in her time, even though she remained virtually
illiterate. A tertiary Dominican nun, she experienced visions
all her life, beginning at the age of six. In a sensational case,
her mystical claims were challenged before the General
Chapter of the Dominicans at Florence, but Catherine was
vindicated. In 1375 on a visit to Pisa she felt the pains of the
stigmata, though the physical signs did not appear on her
hands and feet until after her death. She made a dramatic
appeal to Pope Gregory XI at Avignon, demanding that he

return permanently to Rome, which he did. Back in Siena she dictated an account of her visions. Her death was at Rome, during an unsuccessful attempt to heal the split in the Church known as the Great Schism.

Feast: 29 April
Patron of Italy, Siena, Rome
Shrine: Siena
Symbols in art: crown of thorns, dove, nun's habit
Writings: *The Dialogue of St Catherine*

Cecilia

Virgin and Martyr
2nd century

The musical Cecilia was a Christian Roman noblewoman, but her story is mostly legend. Her singing made angels appear and she is said to have invented the pipe organ. Though secretly dedicated to virginity, she was forcibly married to Valerian, shutting her ears to the orchestra at the wedding feast, and singing 'in her heart alone to the Lord: "Let my heart and my body be undefiled, O Lord, that I may not be confounded"'. That night she converted Valerian by showing him an angel and he agreed to celibacy. He did many good works, including the illegal burial of executed Christians, but was caught and put to death. Cecilia was herself examined, refused to sacrifice to the gods and was condemned to be scalded in a boiling bath. But 'she lay in the bath as in a cool place' before suffering a bungled attempt at decapitation. Lingering in pain for three days, she gave away her wealth to the poor, then died.

Feast: 22 November
Patron of musicians and instrument-makers
Cause: music
Symbols in art: neck wound, chaplet of flowers, musical
  instrument, cauldron
Source: *The Golden Legend*

Charles Borromeo

Bishop and Reformer
1538–84. Canonised 1610

His father a count and his mother the sister of Pope Pius IV, Charles came from a privileged family. He was made secretary of state to his uncle the Pope, and a cardinal at only 22. An outstanding administrator, he organised the final session of the Council of Trent, which launched the Counter-Reformation. He later became Bishop of Milan and instituted reforms at every level of his diocese – causing resentment and even an assassination attempt by a priest. In the plague of 1576–8, he remained in the city after the civil rulers had fled, making great efforts to relieve the people's suffering. He was a patron of the arts and scholarship and overcame a stammer to become a highly effective preacher.

Feast: 4 November
Patron of Roman clergy, spiritual directors, starch-makers
Cause: plague
Shrine: Milan

Christopher

Martyr
3rd century. Reduced to local status 1969

It is impossible to tell how much of the colourful legend of Christopher is fact. Originally a Canaanite called Offero, he was a giant of a man who desired to find a master worthy of his service. His first master was high-born but afraid of the devil. Offero then served the devil but, seeing him trembling at the sight of a cross, decided Christ must be an even greater master and left to search for him. He met a hermit who told him that he might serve Christ by carrying travellers across a nearby torrent, which he did. One stormy night he hoisted a mysterious child on his back who, though small, weighed heavier than any burden he had ever carried. He almost sank under the raging water, but struggled on. Reaching the far side, he planted his staff in the bank to pull

St Christopher by Titian (d.1576) in Venice's
Palazzo Ducale (Dagli Orti)

St Clare of Assisi holding a monstrance, the symbol in art with which she is associated, by Giovanni Battista Moroni (c.1525–78), in the Museo Tridentino Arte Sacra, Trento (Dagli Orti)

himself out and it began to sprout leaves. Only then did he realise his passenger was Jesus. From that time he was Christopher, the Christ-bearer. The medieval Christopher cult was strong, but declined in the 17th century. It has gained new impetus in the age of motor and air travel.

> **Feast:** 25 July
> **Patron of** travellers
> **Cause:** against storms and sudden death
> **Symbol in art:** sprouting staff

Clare of Assisi (Clare Offreduccio)

Visionary and Foundress of the Order of Poor Clares
1194–1253. Canonised 1255

Born and brought up in Assisi, Clare was a pious and strong-minded girl who defied her father's attempt to marry her off at the age of twelve and, six years later, she left home to follow **St Francis**. She was established by the saint as the nucleus and superior of a nunnery adjoining the church of San Damiano, where she lived for the rest of her life. This was the start of the Poor Clares, the austere Order that many believe is a more complete embodiment of Francis's ideas than the male Franciscans. Clare was a charismatic figure who, despite chronic illness, fought hard for the Franciscan principles of absolute poverty and service, a struggle which twice brought her into conflict with the Pope. When Assisi was besieged by Saracen mercenaries in the pay of the king of France, there was a real fear that the Muslim troops would sack the city. The ailing Clare asked to be carried on a litter to the walls, where she showed the enemy the Blessed Sacrament. They dispersed in terror. Her visions, both celestial and infernal, have made her an intercessor against blindness and the patron of television.

Feast: 11 August
Patron of television
Cause: blindness
Shrine: Assisi
Symbol in art: monstrance
Source: The Life of St Clare, ascribed to Thomas of Celano

Columba

Abbot and Missionary
*c.*521–97

Born in Donegal, Columba left Ireland after a row with St Finnian of Moville, whose Psalter he had copied without the saint's permission. Ordered to return both copies to Finnian, Columba sailed in high dudgeon to Iona, off the Isle of Mull. Here he expelled all female creatures in order to establish a celibate community of monks, whose members went out and preached to the heathen Picts. Columba's personal power was impressive – he once outfaced a giant sea creature in the River Ness, which then slunk away into the loch and is the monster still discussed today. Columba, the Rule-giver of Celtic-style monasticism in Scotland and northern England, must have been a highly practical leader, but his legend is one of prophecy, miracle-working and fantastic deeds.

Feast: 9 June
Shrine: Iona
Symbol in art: bear
Source: St Adamnan's *Life of Columba*

Cosmas and Damian

Martyrs
3rd or 4th century

These twins were Christian doctors, originally from Arabia but who settled in Cilicia, offering free medical treatment to all. The Roman governor Lysias heard of their fame and questioned them. Jealous of their popularity and unable to shake their faith, he condemned the twins to death. *The Golden Legend*, which popularised their cult in the Middle Ages, recites a longer than usual catalogue of cruelties – drowning, burning, boiling, shooting, racking and stoning – from which they were preserved before being beheaded.

SS Cosmas and Damian by Fernando del Rincon, in the Museo del Prado, Madrid (Dagli Orti)

A sacristan of their church, after suffering from a gangrenous leg and praying to the saints, found that the diseased limb had been swapped for a healthy one belonging to a recently dead Moor, so that he now had one black and one white leg.

Feast: 26 September
Patron of doctors, barbers, the Medici family of Florence
Causes: medicine, especially hernia and pestilence
Shrine: Church of SS Cosmas and Damian, Rome
Source: *The Golden Legend*

Crispin and Crispinian

Martyrs
3rd century

Said to be a pair of Christian cobblers from Rome who settled at Soissons, France, where they preached the gospels and were eventually martyred. But it may only be their bones that came to France: the relics were at any rate enshrined in a Soissons church by the 6th century. Another story connects them with Faversham in Kent, whose parish church once contained a memorial to them.

Feast: 25 October
Patron of shoemakers, leather-workers
Shrine: Soissons, France
Symbols in art: shoe, last

An illustrated manuscript (c. 1300) entitled St Cuthbert
and Two Brethren Returning from the Land of Picts
in the collection of the British Library

Cuthbert

Bishop
634–87

Cuthbert was a shepherd boy in the Scottish borders who, after experiencing a vision, left his sheep to become a monk at nearby Melrose. He later transferred to St Aidan's Lindisfarne, where he rose to be abbot. Many stories tell of his affinity for the natural world, in addition to his care for his monks and (after he became Bishop of Lindisfarne) his concern for the laity under his authority. He was also drawn to solitude and would go alone to the small islet of Farne to pray and meditate through the night, standing up to his waist in the sea. He was buried at Lindisfarne but, in 875, the monks fled Viking raiders, taking his body with them in a cart. No suitable resting place was found for many years until they came to Durham, where he was buried. In time Cuthbert's relics found their place behind the high altar of Durham's 12th-century cathedral, to be rediscovered in 1827, still in the wooden coffin in which they had travelled from Lindisfarne.

***

Feast: 20 March
Patron of Northern England, Durham, sailors
Shrine: Durham Cathedral
Source: Bede's *Life of Cuthbert*

David

Bishop
d. c.600. Canonised 1120

David's unmarried mother, St Non, gave birth to him during a storm while lying on a granite slab surrounded by megaliths. Educated at the monastery of Yr Henllwyn, he founded twelve abbeys, the most famous at his birthplace in the city named after him. It was to St David's that he brought his headquarters and where his relics are to be found. He is said to have visited Jerusalem and won a debate with the heretic Pelagius. His monasticism placed a high value on everyday acts of kindness and on alcoholic abstention.

Feast: 1 March
Patron of Wales, poets
Shrine: St David's, Pembrokeshire
Symbol in art: dove
Source: Rhygyfarch's *Life of St David*

Denis (Dionysius of Paris)

Bishop and Martyr
d. 258

The Golden Legend confusingly amalgamates this saint with Dionysius of Athens – the 1st-century martyr, mentioned in the Acts of the Apostles as a convert of **St Paul** who was to become Primate of Greece. But the French Denis is a much later figure, hardly known to history. In legend his episcopacy at Paris was terminated with his beheading after the heathen had put him to trial by crucifixion, fire and wild beasts. The execution was at Montmartre ('Martyr's Hill') and the watching crowd was amazed to see his corpse immediately rise up, tuck the severed head under its arm and walk to his chosen burial site, beneath what is now the church of St Denis. It is as a 'cephalophore' or head-carrier that he is usually portrayed.

Feast: 9 October
Patron of France
Causes: against frenzy, headache, social conflict
Shrine: St Denis, Paris
Symbol in art: severed head held in hands
Source: *The Golden Legend*

Dominic

Founder of the Order of Preachers (Black Friars)
1170–1221. Canonised 1234

Born in Castile, Dominic was a canon at the cathedral of Osma until 1203, when his bishop, Diego, chose to take him on a mission to the heretical Albigensians in southern France. The pair evolved a new, more intimate and humble

St Dominic painted by Alonso Florin in 1621, in the
Museo Civico, Correggio (Dagli Orti)

form of proselytising, which Dominic continued after Diego's death, despite the appalling savagery of the Albigensian crusade, launched in 1208 by Pope Innocent III. By 1215 Dominic had worked out his plans for an Order of friars living in poverty under a quasi-monastic rule, but going out to disseminate the gospels to people in all walks of life. The Order was approved in 1216 and, in his last six years, the founder oversaw its expansion into the major cities of Western Europe. He died at Bologna.

Feast: 8 August
Patron of the Order of Preachers
Shrine: San Domenico, Bologna, Italy
Symbols in art: star, dog with a torch between its teeth, devil holding a devotional candle

Dunstan

Bishop
*c.*910–*c.* 988

Dunstan was a political prelate who did much to revive monasticism in the later years of Anglo-Saxon England. Summoned by King Edmund of Wessex in 943 to take charge of Glastonbury Abbey, he turned it into a centre of great learning. He was then one of the chief advisers to Edmund's successor, Edred, and instigated a systematic monastic reform. But in the next reign, as King Edwy's bitter enemy, he was banished to Flanders until Edwy's overthrow, whereupon he became Archbishop of Canterbury and entered into a new partnership with King Edgar, playing a leading role in public life for the next 16 years. As the throne changed hands twice more, Dunstan's influence waned and he retired to Canterbury, where he died. An excellent amateur metalworker and musician, he reputedly composed the hymn '*Kyrie Rex Splendens*'.

Feast: 19 May
Patron of armourers, blacksmiths, goldsmiths, jewellers, locksmiths, musicians, singers
Shrine: St Dunstan's Church, Canterbury
Symbols in art: devil seized by the nose with pincers, dove

Dympna

Martyr
d. *c.*650

Dympna's story was probably adapted from a pre-Christian folk tale to account for bones found at Gheel, near Antwerp, in the 13th century. Allegedly the daughter of a pagan Celtic baron, Dympna was the object of her father's insane sexual passion. With the help of an aged confessor she fled to an oratory at Gheel but her father tracked her down and had the priest killed. When she refused to return with him, he beheaded Dympna himself. The shrine became a resort for those suffering from diabolic possession and nervous diseases, and is now a large centre for the treatment of mental illness. The saint is still remembered in Ireland and the US. In art, Dympna's father is sometimes portrayed as a Saracen.

Feast: 15 May
Patron of epileptics
Causes: insanity, demonic possession
Shrine: St Dympna's Church, Gheel, Belgium
Symbols in art: sword, demon held by a chain
Source: Peter of Cambrai's *Life of St Dympna*

Edmund Campion

Martyr
1540–81. Canonised 1970

Campion was the son of a London bookseller and the most brilliant of those who attempted to turn England back to Catholicism during Elizabeth I's reign. With Robert Persons, he was the first Jesuit to be sent on the perilous English mission in 1580 and was thought so dangerous that the penal law was strengthened and one of the greatest manhunts ever seen in England launched. For a while

Campion eluded capture and, in a daring piece of
subversion, copies of his tract *Ten Reasons* were placed in
every pew of the Oxford University church before an
important service. In 1581 Campion was caught, but neither
persuasion nor torture could induce him to recant. He was
hanged, drawn and quartered at Tyburn on 1 December and
received canonisation under Pope Paul VI with the other '40
Martyrs of England and Wales'.

> **Feast:** 1 December
> **Shrines:** Tyburn Convent, Marble Arch, London; Campion
> Hall, Oxford

Edward the Confessor

King
1004–66. Canonised 1161

Born at Islip, Oxfordshire, the son of an English king and a
Norman princess, Edward lived in England and Normandy
before ascending the English throne at the age of 37. His
reign, in a turbulent era, was unusually peaceful and he
enjoyed a reputation for piety and good works, though his
unwarlike nature was despised by Norman historians.

An illuminated manuscript of Edward the
Confessor at the Easter Banquet

Edward built the first Westminster Abbey and is the originator of the traditional ability of English kings to cure scrofula, the King's Evil, with a touch. He is the only English king to be recognised by the Church as a saint.

Feast: 13 October
Cause: scrofula
Shrine: relics in Westminster Abbey, London
Symbol in art: finger ring
Source: *The Life of St Edward the Confessor*

Elizabeth and Zachary

Parents of John the Baptist
1st century

Zachary was a temple priest, and Elizabeth the first cousin of the Virgin **Mary**. According to Luke's gospel the couple were 'well stricken in years' when the Archangel Gabriel told them that Elizabeth would bear her first child, whose name he specified. Zachary could not believe this and for his lack of faith he was struck dumb. Six months later, after the Annunciation, **Mary** visited Elizabeth, whose child 'leaped in her womb'. Subsequently, when **John the Baptist** was born his parents rejected a family name, despite relatives' protests. Zachary called for a tablet to write 'his name is John' and, at this, his tongue was loosed.

Feast: 5 November
Symbol: censer
Source: Luke I

Elizabeth of Hungary

Queen
1207–31. Canonised 1235

Elizabeth was the daughter of King Andrew II of Hungary and wife of Ludwig IV of Thuringia. Her husband, with whom she had been very happy for six years, died on the journey to the Crusades. Her brother-in-law then evicted her from her castle and she withdrew to become a tertiary Franciscan at Marburg, where she devoted herself to the poor and sick. Under the almost brutal spiritual direction of her confessor, Conrad, she was severely tested but kept her resolve to serve the needy until her death at only 24. She has always been one of the most popular of German saints.

Feast: 19 November
Patron of bakers, beggars, lacemakers, charities
Cause: toothache
Shrine: Saragossa, Spain
Symbol in art: basket of roses

Elizabeth (Isabel) of Portugal

Queen
1271–1336. Canonised 1626

The great niece of **St Elizabeth of Hungary**, this saint married King Denis of Portugal at the age of twelve and together they had two children. Denis was a strong king but also a hard and unfaithful husband. The couple's son, Alfonso, as a young man rose up in revolt and Denis suspected that Elizabeth might be involved. In fact her efforts had always been patiently directed towards reconciliation, but he had her imprisoned nevertheless. Suffering this uncomplainingly, Elizabeth became a 'Poor Clare' after Denis's death in 1325, but returned to the world for one last time when her son declared war on Castile. Ultimately, her peacemaking efforts were successful, but they had worn her out and she died the same year.

> **Feast:** 4 July
> **Shrine:** Estremoz, Portugal
> **Symbol in art:** rose

Elizabeth Seton

Foundress
1774–1821. Canonised 1975

This New Yorker was the first American-born saint to be canonised. Originally an Episcopalian and daughter of a medical professor, she married an anatomist, Richard Seton, and had five children before his death in 1803. She became a Catholic, to the disgust of her family, and in 1809 founded a small religious community and a school for the poor near Emmitsburg, Maryland, America's first Catholic parochial school. Her community's Rule was approved in 1812, becoming the Sisters of Charity, of which she was the first superior. Despite her excellent education, she had to overcome chronic self-doubts about her leadership, as well as moments of severe spiritual desolation.

Feast: 4 January
Writings: *Letters to Mrs J. Scott*

Etheldreda (Audrey)

Abbess and Virgin
630–79

Born at Exning, Suffolk, Etheldreda was of royal blood. Although married twice, she succeeded in retaining her virginity, which severely tried her second husband, King Egfrid of Northumbria, who eventually sent her to a nunnery, an act approved by **St Wilfrid**. Etheldreda went on to found a community on the remote Isle of Ely which she led with much of the same authority and charisma as her contemporary **St Hilda of Whitby**. She died of throat cancer, which she said was retribution for her youthful love of fine neckwear, and her bones lie in Ely Cathedral. Etheldreda became one of the great female saints of England, with Ely as a major pilgrimage centre. On her feast day, St Audrey's Fair sold cheap ribbons and beads ('tawdry') with which pilgrims decorated the shrine.

Feast: 23 June
Patron of Cambridge University
Cause: diseases of the throat
Shrines: Ely Cathedral; St Etheldreda's Chapel, Ely Place,
  London
Source: Bede's *History of England*, Hymn to St Audrey

Fiacre (Fiachra)

Hermit
d. *c.*670

An Irish hermit, Fiacre went to France, where
St Faro granted him some land as a hermitage,
which Fiacre cultivated and fiercely defended against
encroachment by females. He also established a hospice
nearby. His shrine at Meaux attracted the sick throughout
the Middle Ages and was especially efficacious against piles.
The first horsedrawn cab in Paris plied its trade from the
Hôtel St-Fiacre from 1620.

Feast: 30 August (1 September in Ireland and France)
Patron of gardeners and cab drivers
Cause: haemorrhoids
Shrines: St Fiacre-en-Brie; Meaux, France
Symbol in art: spade

Finnian of Clonard

Abbot and Founder
470–549

Possibly born in County Carlow, Finnian studied in Wales under SS Cadoc and Gilda before returning to found the Irish monastic tradition. He established a huge foundation at Clonard, County Meath, where both **St Columba** and **St Brendan** came to study. This Finnian, who died of plague, is not to be confused with St Finnian of Moville, importer of the first copy of **St Jerome**'s Latin Psalter to Ireland. It is this book of which **St Columba** made an unauthorised and much disputed copy.

Feast: 12 December
Shrine: Clonard, County Meath

Francis of Assisi (Giovanni Francesco Bernadone)

Founder of the Franciscan Order
1181–1226. Canonised 1228

Francis is one of the great figures of world history and no one but Christ has done more to awaken Christianity's social conscience. In a vision, the 24-year-old son of a rich Assisi

St Francis of Assisi by Pomponio Amalteo
(Dagli Orti)

draper received God's command to 'repair my Church' and this set him on a lifetime ministry of radical poverty. After a public break with his father, Francis's passion soon attracted disciples and in 1210 his group was authorised by the Pope for itinerant preaching. From this grew the Friars Minor, a popular movement to regenerate Christ's concern for poverty and the poor, although the brothers needed constant reminders of this commitment. Francis's patronage of nature comes from his concern for all of creation and he is often portrayed preaching to the birds. In 1224 he received the stigmata.

Feast: 4 October
Patron of Assisi, ecologists
Cause: renunciation
Shrine: Assisi
Symbols in art: birds, deer, fish, skull, stigmata, wolf
Writings: *The Canticle of the Sun*
Source: *Lives* by St Bonaventure and Thomas of Celano, *Little Flowers of St Francis*, Anon

---

Francis of Sales

Bishop and Doctor of the Church
1567–1622. Canonised 1665. Doctor 1877

Francis was a Savoyard who studied law at Padua. Rejecting the chance of a brilliant secular career, he was ordained in

St Francis of Sales painted by Giambattista Tiepolo (1696–1770), from the collection of the Museo Civico, Udine (Dagli Orti)

1593, and was sent to Geneva, a hotbed of Calvinism, where his preaching was so successful that he was constantly threatened by mobs and assassins. Promoted to Bishop of Geneva in 1602, he became one of the great men of the Counter Reformation, with a style sharply distinct from the Jesuits' penitential severity. Francis mapped a path to holiness through everyday life and his spirituality had a gentleness and psychological insight that won him many followers. With one of these, St Jeanne Françoise de Chantal, he founded the Order of the Visitation. His books are spiritual classics and are still read today.

Feast: 24 January
Patron of journalists and writers
Shrine: Annecy, France
Writings: *Introduction to the Devout Life* (1609); *Treatise on the Love of God* (1616)

Francis Xavier

Missionary
1506–1552. Canonised 1622

Francis became a follower of his fellow Spanish Basque **St Ignatius of Loyola** while studying in Paris and was among the first group of seven Jesuits to take vows at Montmartre in 1534. In 1542 he arrived in Portuguese Goa on his

A detail from a portal of the University College, Granada, Spain, built in 1590, showing St Francis Xavier baptising an Indian (Dagli Orti)

famous mission to India and achieved notable success with local converts while denouncing the immorality of the colonists. He extended his mission around the South China Sea and to Japan, but his greatest wish was to evangelise China itself, then closed to foreigners. He died within sight of his goal, a few hours after landing from a boat on an island off the Chinese coast.

Feast: 3 December
Patron of India, overseas missions
Cause: the Conversion of the East
Shrine: Goa
Writings: letters, of which many survive

Frideswide

Virgin and Foundress
d. *c.*735

The daughter of a king of Mercia, Frideswide had no taste for marriage and rejected the advances of her fiancé, who was struck blind until he desisted. She became an anchorite at Binsey, near Oxford, where a miraculous well appeared which can still be seen (*see* **St Margaret of Antioch**). Around her a religious community gathered which evolved into an abbey and then the cathedral of Christ Church, Oxford. Frideswide's bones were rediscovered during Queen Mary's reign but disposed by Elizabethan Protestants.

Feast: 19 October
Patron of the City of Oxford
Cause: blindness, either moral or physical
Shrines: Christ Church, Oxford; the village of Bomy, France

Geneviève of Paris

Religious
422–500

Geneviève was born at Nanterre and known
for her piety from the age of seven. Her mother
was struck blind after boxing Geneviève's ears but
was cured by water her daughter had blessed. The saint
took the veil in Paris at 15 and clearly had remarkable
visionary powers, attracting enemies as well as followers.
But her accurate prophecies gave her authority and she is
remembered for saving the city from Attila the Hun and
from the plague of 1129. In Paris she built the church of St
Denis as well as the church now named after her.

Feast: 3 January
Patron of Paris
Shrines: St Geneviève and St Etienne du Mont, Paris
Symbols in art: candle, book, shepherd's crook

George

Soldier and Martyr
3rd century. Reduced to local status 1969

The very existence of St George was questioned as early as the 5th century but, for a figure so obscure, his cult is vigorous and widespread. Said to have been a Roman officer, he delivered a village in Libya from a malevolent dragon, which afterwards followed him everywhere like a dog. He was eventually martyred under Diocletian and was venerated throughout the early Eastern Church. In the West his cult took off with *The Golden Legend*, and his association with knighthood, such an important idea after the Crusades. In the 14th century, he displaced the more mundane figure of **St Edward the Confessor** as England's national saint.

Feast: 23 April
Patron of England, Portugal, Germany, Aragon, Venice, Genoa, Barcelona, soldiers, Boy Scouts, farmers
Causes: warfare, chivalry, agriculture
Shrine: Lydda, Palestine
Symbols in art: white flag with red cross, dragon, lance

A 16th-century representation of St George in the
Recklinghausen Museum

Giles (Aegidius)

Hermit
d. *c.*712

Giles was born in Athens, where his piety and
miracles brought him a renown he did not relish
Escaping, he tried to reach Rome, but landed in France,
where he lived as a hermit. He was shot by a hunter's arrow
shielding a doe that had given him milk, but survived and
went on to found the abbey of St Giles and become
confessor to Charlemagne. His cult was strong all over
medieval Europe, where he was seen as one who, if he
absolved an emperor, would not refuse absolution to anyone.

Feast: 1 September
Patron of Edinburgh, beggars, the disabled, the woods
Causes: physical handicap, confession, fear of the dark
Shrine: Abbaye de St-Gilles du Gard, Arles
Symbols in art: arrow, doe, crozier, lily

Gregory the Great

Pope and Father of the Church
540–604. Canonised 604

Gregory was a wealthy Roman who grew up at a time of
prolonged disorder, during which Emperor Justinian's

reconquest of Italy was pushed back by new Gothic invasions. Gregory became a priest and turned his family estate into a flourishing Benedictine monastery. Although both ugly and sickly, he was promoted to Pope's secretary and then, in 590, to the papacy. His 14-year pontificate was arguably the most seminal in Church history. He expanded Rome's influence into northern Europe (notably Britain), reformed the Church's finances, universalised the liturgy and its musical language and laid the foundations of the papal bureaucracy, the Curia. Hundreds of his letters survive and his thought left a deep mark on theology. He defined the Pope as 'the servant of the servants of God'.

Feast: 3 September (formerly 12 March)
Patron of singers, teachers
Symbols in art: dove (denoting the Holy Spirit), crozier, mitre
Writings: *Regula Pastoralis* ('Pastoral Care'), *Moralia*, *Dialogues*

Gwen Teirbron

Mother
5th century

One of the many saints whose history has clearly merged with pre-Christian legends, the Breton St Gwen was reputed to have been miraculously endowed with three breasts to suckle her triplets, Guenole, Jaccut and Vennec, who all grew up to become notable Breton saints. Her shrines were attacked by the zealous Breton clergy in the 1870s and many of her images were broken. In the British Isles she was venerated as St White, Wita or Candida.

Feast: 1 June
Patron of nursing mothers
Cause: breastfeeding
Shrine: various throughout Brittany
Symbol in art: three-breasted woman

Helena

Mother of Emperor Constantine
*c.*250–*c.*330

In legend the Emperor Constantine's mother was of noble British birth; in reality she was the daughter of an innkeeper in Asia Minor. But she married General Constantius Chlorus, who later became emperor and was succeeded by their son. Converted to Christianity with Constantine, she is most famous for her journey in 327 to the Holy Land where, according to various 4th-century sources, she found the True Cross buried close to Calvary. Her porphyry sarcophagus survives in the Vatican Museum.

St Helena Interrogating a Jew *by Martin Bernat and Miguel Jimenez, in the Zaragoza Museum, Spain (Dagli Orti)*

Feast: 18 August
Shrine: Trier Cathedral, Germany
Symbols in art: cross, nails

Henry II

Emperor
973–1024. Canonised 1146

As Duke of Bavaria from 995, Henry was already a powerful figure when he was elected Holy Roman Emperor in 1002 (and crowned in 1014). Despite his professed desire to live as a monk, he was a bold and successful ruler, not shrinking from use of arms to increase the unity and strength of the German nations. He was also austere and religious and is perhaps the most powerful temporal ruler ever to achieve sainthood. His wife, Cunegund, was also canonised.

Feast: 13 July
Shrine: Bamberg Cathedral, Germany

Hilda of Whitby

Abbess
614–80

A royal princess, Hilda was abbess at Hartlepool, on **St Aidan**'s recommendation, before running the abbey of

Whitby, founded by King Oswy of Northumbria to mark his victory over paganism. Under her direction Whitby – a house with foundations for men and women – became one of the most advanced centres of learning in Britain. Here she convened the Synod of Whitby (661) to resolve the rival claims of the Celtic and Roman liturgies. To her disappointment, the Roman triumphed, sealing the fate of Hilda's Celtic-style monasticism. Almost two hundred years after her death, Danes destroyed the abbey but, two hundred years on, the site became the Benedictine house whose ruins can still be seen.

Feast: 17 November
Shrine: Whitby Abbey, North Yorkshire
Source: Bede's *History of England*

Hugh of Lincoln

Bishop
1140–1200. Canonised 1220

Hugh was born in Avalon, Burgundy, and lived the obscure life of a Carthusian monk for 17 years, but word of his abilities seeped out and in 1178 he was summoned to take charge of the new charterhouse, the first in England. Founded by King Henry II as part of his penance for the murder of **Thomas à Becket**, Hugh built and ran the charterhouse with dry good humour and astuteness. In 1186 he was unwillingly promoted to the see of Lincoln, where he built the cathedral and showed there was a sound administrator beneath his spirituality. One of the most unassuming great men of his age, Hugh's courage was such that he outfaced anti-Semitic lynch mobs and openly criticised the extremely prickly king.

Feast: 17 November
Shrine: Lincoln Cathedral
Symbols in art: swan, cup containing a child

Ignatius of Loyola

Founder of the Society of Jesus
1491–1556. Canonised 1622

Ignatius was a Basque nobleman and a soldier. Seriously wounded during the French siege of Pamplona, he saw the vanity of war and decided to refocus his military instincts towards God's service. A decade's study and meditation led to his taking vows at Montmartre in Paris with a group of followers (including **St Francis Xavier**) – the inaugural Jesuits. Under his leadership, ultimately based in Rome, the Society grew to dominate Catholic education and missionary work, its priest members nurtured by Ignatius's *Spiritual Exercises* and bound by a vow of total obedience to the Pope. They became the 'shock troops' of the

Counter-Reformation in Europe and spearheaded the Catholic overseas expansion into the Orient and South America.

Feast: 31 July
Patron of Jesuits, soldiers
Shrine: the Gesu Church, Rome
Writings: *The Spiritual Exercises, Autobiography, Spiritual Diary, Letters*

Isidore of Seville

Bishop and Doctor of the Church
560–636. Canonised 1598. Doctor of the Church 1722

An industrious figure of the early Spanish Church, Isidore summoned councils, proselytised the Visigoths, combated Arianism, founded schools and monasteries and wrote voluminously. His most ambitious contribution to learning was his *Etymologies*, an early encyclopaedia which attempted to summarise all existing knowledge.

Feast: 4 April
Patron of the Internet (proposed)
Shrine: cathedral at León, Spain
Symbols in art: bishop's mitre, crozier
Writings: *Etymologies, History of Goths* and *Vandals*, numerous other works

Isidore the Ploughman

Layman
1070–1130. Canonised 1622

A stalwart labourer, Isidore worked all his life on the land near Madrid. Once he was refused permission to stop ploughing to say his prayers and, when the farmer checked up on his employee, he found Isidore on his knees in the field while two angels drove the plough. His cult grew large in Spain, where many miracles were attributed to his intercession.

Feast: 15 May
Patron of Cathedral of St Isidore, Madrid, farmers
Shrine: Madrid
Symbols in art: sickle, sheaf of corn

James the Great

Apostle and Martyr
1st century

Shortly after **Andrew** and Simon **Peter** were called to follow Christ, James, with his younger brother, **John the Evangelist**, was mending fishing nets on Lake Genesaret with their father, Zebedee, when Christ came down to the shore and summoned them also. James

St James the Great by El Greco (1541–1614), in the
Museo de Santa Cruz (Joseph Martin)

was one of the inner circle of Apostles and was present at such key moments as the Transfiguration and the Agony in the Garden. He later became the first of the disciples to be martyred, beheaded by Herod Agrippa because 'it pleased the Jews'. The story that he travelled to Spain, and performed many miracles there, is not credible, although some of his relics may have done. Santiago de Compostela – where they are said to be – has been one of the world's most popular pilgrimage sites for more than a thousand years.

Feast: 25 July
Patron of Spain
Cause: rheumatism
Shrine: Santiago de Compostela, Spain
Symbols in art: cockleshell, bear hitched to a plough, key, sword

James the Less

Apostle and Martyr
1st century

James, son of Alpheus, is called the Less to distinguish him from the son of Zebedee, who was called the Great. This James has usually been identified with **James**, 'brother of the Lord', who looked so like Christ that the Judas kiss was necessary in the Garden of Gethsemane to pick out the Lord. He is traditionally the son of the Virgin **Mary's** half-sister, making him Christ's cousin. After the Ascension, James governed the Jerusalem Church for many years and was martyred by stoning.

Feast: 3 May
Patron of fullers, hatters
Symbol in art: fuller's staff
Writings: The Epistle of James

Jerome (Eusebius Hieronymus Sophronius)

Father of the Church
342–420

Jerome was born in Dalmatia to parents who
were prosperous, and at least one of them was
Christian. His long career was varied and he was at different
times a monk, desert ascetic, scholar, author, controversialist
and Pope's secretary. More importantly, his Latin translation
of scripture from the original tongues created the Vulgate
Bible, the approved Catholic text until the 20th century. By
tradition Jerome was a man torn between his Christian faith
and love of classical authors. A lion from whose paw he
drew a thorn was his legendary desert companion.

Feast: 30 September
Patron of students
Shrine: Church of the Nativity, Bethlehem
Symbols in art: book, cardinal's hat, lion
Writings: many tracts and diatribes, Bible translated into
Latin

St Jerome and the Lion *by Niccolo*
Colantino (c.1450)

Joan of Arc

Mystic, Soldier and Martyr
1412–31. Canonised 1920

The Maid of Orléans was born in the Meuse valley during the Hundred Years War and, for a heady few months, this illiterate peasant girl of no more than 20 was the military and political power in France. As a child she had heard the insistent voices of **SS Margaret of Antioch**, **Catherine of Alexandria** and **Michael**, telling her to raise the siege of Orléans and save the vacant French throne. Obtaining an audience with the Dauphin Charles in 1429, she convinced him to give her armour and a horse and she led his troops in a successful attack. After more victories, Charles VII was crowned at Rheims but the next year Joan was captured in battle by the Burgundians, who sold her to the English at Rouen. She was tried and publicly burned as a witch, a process condemned by the Pope in 1456 as fraudulent.

Feast: 30 May
Patron of France
Shrines: Rouen; Orléans

Joan of Arc, painted by Dominique Ingres (1780–1867) in 1854, held in the Musée du Louvre, Paris (Dagli Orti)

John Chrysostom

Doctor of the Church
347–407. Canonised 451

Chrysostom means 'golden-mouthed', a tribute to his preaching at Antioch, where he was born and studied and where he worked for twelve years under Bishop Flavian. His expositions of the New Testament made him famous throughout Asia Minor and by 398 he was Patriarch of Constantinople. As a reformer, opposed to luxury, sensuality and idolatry, he made enemies. In 404 he was deposed and exiled to Cucusus in Armenia, where he wrote over two hundred letters. As controversy about his treatment raged, he died on his way to a more remote banishment at the eastern end of the Black Sea. Legend has it that he did penance for a sexual affair by crawling naked on all fours like an animal.

Feast: 13 September (previously 27 January)
Patron of preachers
Shrine: Constantinople
Symbol in art: a Byzantine church
Writings: letters and sermons, *Treatise on the Priesthood*

John Fisher

Bishop and Martyr
1469–1535. Canonised 1935

A Yorkshireman from Beverley, Fisher was Bishop of Rochester and a brilliant but deeply conservative Catholic churchman. In 1534 his doctrinal obduracy met an even greater stubbornness in King Henry VIII of England. Henry wanted to divorce Katherine of Aragon and was prepared to make himself head of the Church to do so. Fisher opposed this with passionate but lucid arguments, finally refusing to accept the Bill of Succession, which usurped the prerogative of the Pope by dissolving Henry's marriage. The bishop now faced trumped-up charges of treason. He was convicted and beheaded on Tower Hill, sharing the fate, a fortnight later, of his friend **Thomas More**.

Feast: 22 June
Writings: *Three Treatises against Luther*

John of God

Founder of the Order of Brothers Hospitallers
1495–1550. Canonised 1690

After absconding from his parents' house in Portugal and leading a roistering life as a soldier and slave-driver, the

middle-aged John was inspired to repent by the preaching of
St John of Avila at Granada. So extreme were his
expressions of penitence that he was imprisoned as a lunatic.
On recovering his reason, he set about providing
accommodation for the sick and dispossessed. The Order
which now bears John's name was consolidated after his
death and has spread to many countries.

Feast: 8 March
Patron of nurses, the sick, hospitals, booksellers, printers
Cause: hospital medicine
Shrine: Granada, Spain

John of the Cross (Juan de Yepes y Alvarez)

Poet, Mystic and Theologian
1542–91. Canonised 1726. Doctor of the Church 1926

An educated Castilian, John allied with Carmelite **St Teresa
of Avila** to reform their Order. Persecution came at first
from the unreformed Order, whose prior general he had
imprisoned on suspicion of heresy. Later the reformed
Cistercians consigned him to an obscure monastery at La
Punuela, where, already ill, he died. One of the greatest
Spanish poets, John expressed mystical experience through
a unique balance of sensual and spiritual language.

Feast: 14 December
Writings: *The Canticle of the Spirit, The Dark Night of the Soul, The Living Flame of Love*

John the Baptist

Prophet
1st century

John is the last of the biblical prophets and the harbinger of the Messiah. Son of **SS Elizabeth and Zachary**, he was six months older than his second cousin Jesus and made his reputation earlier, as preacher and wild man of the desert, where he ate honey and locusts. His symbolic washing of his followers in the Jordan inaugurated the sacrament of baptism and, when Jesus came to him for this purpose, John recognised and proclaimed him as the 'Lamb of God'. The first four Apostles were drawn from the Baptist's circle. John, meanwhile, denounced the incestuous marriage of Herod Antipas and his sister-in-law Herodias and was imprisoned. The queen conspired with her daughter, Salome, to have him beheaded and his head brought to Salome on a dish. The Baptist's relics are scarce, as the emperor is said to have burnt his bones in the 4th century to discourage the cult. John's head rests in Damascus's Omayyad Mosque, where his church once stood.

*John the Baptist by Andrea del Sarto in the
Palazzo Pitti, Florence (Dagli Orti)*

Feast: 24 June
Patron of Turin, Genoa, Florence
Cause: baptism
Shrines: Omayyad Mosque, Damascus; St John Lateran, Rome
Symbols in art: reed cross, lamb, honeycomb, axe, pelt tunic, baptismal cup

John the Evangelist

Apostle
1st century

The most intellectual and visionary of the original Apostles, John is usually identified as the son of Zebedee, a Galilean fisherman who joined Jesus with his brother **St James the Great**. He is not named in his own gospel but referred to as the disciple whom Jesus loved. John is present at most of the key moments in Christ's ministry, including his trial and execution, and, at the foot of the cross, the Virgin **Mary** is committed to his care. In tradition he went to Rome, miraculously escaping martyrdom in a vat of boiling oil. He was then exiled to the Aegean island of Patmos, where he had a remarkable vision of the Apocalypse. He died at Ephesus at the age of about a hundred. Of the gospels, his is the most literary, the most vivid and the most likely to have been written from experience.

An illuminated manuscript of St John the Evangelist,
dating from c.1270, in the British Library

Feast: 27 December
Patron of booksellers
Shrine: Efes (Ephesus), Turkey
Symbols in art: eagle, book, scroll, pen and ink, chalice, cauldron, the Virgin's palm
Writings: Gospel of John, *The Book of Revelation*, three Epistles

John-Baptist Vianney (The Curé of Ars)

Priest
1786–1859. Canonised 1926

A considerable cult arose around this obscure priest, even in his own lifetime. He was a shepherd boy who struggled with his studies and was often mocked for his stupidity and lack of theology. But as priest in the unglamorous parish of Ars-sur-Formans, near Lyons, where he served for 40 years, he was prized as a holy man, an uncomplicated preacher and, above all, a confessor of genius, who could look deeply into the penitent's soul. His spreading fame – and the shrine to **St Philomena** which he built – made Ars a place of pilgrimage where Vianney spent up to 18 hours a day in the confessional. Despite three attempts to retire to a monastery, he was each time recalled to his parish by public demand. His spiritual life was tormented by diabolic visions.

Feast: 8 August
Patron of parish priests (1929)
Cause: the sacrament of penance
Shrine: Ars-sur-Formans, Lyons, France

Joseph

Husband of the Virgin Mary
1st century

In an attempt to explain his sexual continence with **Mary**, and the fact that he disappears so early from the gospels, Joseph is normally represented as an old man. He plays an essential role in accepting Mary's unexplained pregnancy and in protecting and nurturing the young Jesus, who was his apprentice as a carpenter at Nazareth, Galilee, where Joseph had settled from his tribal home in Judaea. Devotion to him was strong in the East from as far back as the 4th century but was not to take off in the West for another millennium and he did not enter the Roman calendar until 1479. His cult has flourished since, to the extent that he now has two feast days.

Feast: 19 March (as 'Husband of Mary'), 1 May (as 'Joseph the Worker')
Patron of Mexico, Canada, the Universal Church (1870), workers (1955)
Symbol in art: pilgrim's staff, carpenter's tools, lily

St Joseph by Francisco de Goya y Lucientes (1746–1828) in the
Zaragoza Museum, Spain (Dagli Orti)

Joseph Mkasa

Martyr (first of the '22 Martyrs of Uganda')
1860–85. Canonised 1964

Joseph, a 25-year-old Catholic, served the despotic King Mwanga of Uganda and was in charge of the young pages at his court. But Mwanga was a brutal paedophile and Joseph – the foremost in a group of about two hundred Christians at the court – earned his enmity by denouncing the king's immorality. In November 1885 Joseph was beheaded. A violent purge followed, including the burning alive of 32 Christians at Namugongo, many of them Joseph's pages.

Feast: 3 June
Cause: against child abuse
Shrine: Namugongo, Uganda

Joseph of Arimathea

Disciple
1st century

A secret disciple of Christ in Jerusalem, Joseph was a man of means. He was present at the crucifixion and, in legend, collected drops of the Holy Blood in the chalice (grail) that had been used at the

Last Supper. He obtained Christ's body from Pilate and, with Nicodemus, was responsible for preparing it for entombment in Joseph's own tomb, using a large quantity of expensive unguents. A medieval legend has him travelling with **St Philip** to Gaul and from there, in 63 BC, to England, where he carried the grail to Glastonbury and buried it under a thornbush said to have sprouted from Joseph's walking stick. A church of wattles was built and here Joseph was buried.

Feast: 17 March
Shrine: Glastonbury
Symbols in art: shroud, crown of thorns, nails

Jude (Thaddeus)

Apostle and Martyr
1st century

Whether or not the Apostle Jude, also called Thaddeus, was the author of the 'Letter of St Jude' is uncertain. Equally obscure is whether he and **Simon the Zealot** were both sons of Alpheus and brothers of **James the Less**, as *The Golden Legend* insists. Jude is said to have gone to Edessa with Simon, and later preached in Mesopotamia, Pontus and Persia, where he and Simon contended with wizards before being martyred. Because his name so closely resembled Judas, he was rarely invoked except by those whose causes were almost hopeless.

Feast: 28 October (with St Simon the Zealot)
Cause: desperate circumstances
Symbols in art: club, halberd, lance, set square

Julian Hospitaller ('The Poor Man')

An entirely mythical but very popular figure in the Middle Ages. Known through a story in *The Golden Legend*, Julian appears as a nobleman, told by a miraculous stag that he would kill his parents. Some time later, after mistaking their identities, he committed the murder and in expiation he and his wife founded a hospice for poor travellers at a river ford. On one occasion he rescued a leper from the cold water, who transformed into an angel and told him that his penance was acceptable.

Feast: 12 February
Patron of hoteliers, travellers, boatmen, ferrymen, circus performers
Cause: hospitality
Symbols in art: falcon, drawn sword, oar, stag

Lawrence

Martyr
d. 258

Born in Huesca, Aragon, and one of the 'seven deacons of Rome', Lawrence was ordered by the Emperor Valerian's prefect to hand over the church's valuables. He assembled some beggars, saying they were the church's treasures. For his insolence he was put to death by being roasted on a grid, and is said to have joked that he was ready to be turned over for cooking on his other side. He was buried at the site of Rome's St Lawrence Without-the-Walls and, from the 4th century, was one of the most venerated Roman martyrs.

Feast: 10 August
Patron of Sri Lanka, the poor, cooks and chefs
Shrine: St Lawrence Without-the-Walls, Rome
Symbols in art: gridiron, deacon's dalmatic

Leo the Great

Pope and Doctor of the Church
d. 461. Doctor of the Church 1754

Elected Pope in 440, Leo was instrumental in resolving several important doctrinal disputes, especially the monophysite heresy, which he effectively defeated at the Council of Chalcedon (449) by establishing the orthodoxy of Christ's 'two natures in one'. He negotiated personally with Attila the Hun and bribed him to withdraw from Roman territory, but could do nothing about the Vandal entry into Rome in 455, although he did limit the destruction. Leo's permanent legacy was the political view he took of the Papacy, and he greatly strengthened its temporal as well as its spiritual dominion.

Feast: 10 November
Writings: letters and sermons

Louis IX of France

King
1214–70. Canonised 1297

Inheriting the throne of France at the age of twelve, Louis gave much prosperity and peace to the realm. He strengthened feudal institutions and consolidated his power in several regions where it was weak or disputed. As a soldier and statesman he could be both tough and generous and had great integrity. He twice embarked on Crusades. In 1250 he was defeated and captured by the Saracens but ransomed himself. Twenty years later he was not so lucky, dying of dysentery at Tunis.

Louis IX of France by El Greco (1541–1614),
in the collection of Musée du Louvre, Paris (Dagli Orti)

He was a tertiary Franciscan and rebuilt the Ste-Chapelle in Paris to house Christ's crown of thorns, which had been presented to him in 1239.

Feast: 25 August
Patron of protectors of France
Shrine: Ste-Chapelle, Paris
Symbols in art: crown, crown of thorns

Lucy

Virgin and Martyr
d. *c.*304

A virgin of Syracuse, Sicily, Lucy was perhaps martyred during Diocletian's persecutions. As with other Christian virgins, she was denounced for refusing to marry a pagan suitor and initially sentenced to a brothel. She was miraculously preserved from this fate and an attempt to burn her similarly failed. Finally she was stabbed through the throat after having had her eyes put out.

Feast: 13 December
Patron of the blind, cutlers
Causes: ophthalmic disease, spiritual enlightenment
Symbol in art: eyes in a dish

Luke the Evangelist

Apostle
1st century

Luke was a physician, painter and close friend of **St Paul**. He led the Christians at Philippi, in between travelling with Paul on his second and third missions. After Paul's death he went to Greece and is said to have died at the age of 84. His gospel lacks credibility, since it is based on second-hand sources. It is the most readable, however, and is the only source for the Christmas story, the Prodigal Son, the raising of Lazarus and the good Samaritan. Legend insists Luke painted a portrait of the Virgin **Mary**. His winged ox is the conventional symbol, taken from Ezekiel 1: 5–14 and Revelation 4: 6–8.

Feast: 18 October
Patron of artists and their guilds, physicians
Symbol in art: winged ox
Writings: Gospel of Luke, Acts of the Apostles

Madeleine-Sophie Barat

Foundress
1779–1865. Canonised 1925

The daughter of a cooper from Joigny in Burgundian France, Madeleine-Sophie was given a rigorous religious

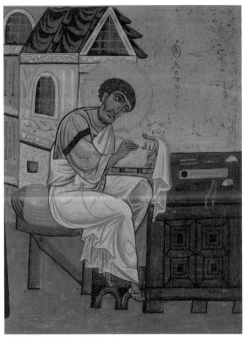

Luke the Evangelist in the Biblioteca
Nazionale Marciana, Venice (Dagli Orti)

education by her ascetic older brother. His friend Joseph
Varin was superior of the Sacred Heart fathers, an
educational group close in spirit to the Jesuits, and he
wanted to launch a women's equivalent. In the young
Madeleine Sophie he found an ideal leader and she became
superior of the Order. During her 63 years in charge, the
Sacred Heart nuns grew to be among the greatest teaching
Orders with more than a hundred schools and houses in
twelve countries. Their foundress was noted for her good
sense, tact and charm, underpinned by unwavering faith.

Feast: 25 May
Patron of the Religious Society of the Sacred Heart
Shrine: Amiens

Margaret of Antioch (Marina)

Virgin and Martyr

A legendary saint popular in the Middle Ages, Margaret fled
her pagan father, becoming a shepherdess. For spurning the
advances of the prefect Olybrius she was arrested as a
Christian and, in prison, was visited by a devil-dragon. It
swallowed her whole but she proved indigestible and was
disgorged – the origin of her patronage of childbirth.
Elaborate attempts to kill her failed before she was

*St Margaret of Antioch by Francisco de Zurbarán
(1598–1664) in the National Gallery, London*

beheaded. Margaret's legend is often confused with that of an ex-belly-dancer called Pelagia or Margarita the Penitent.

Feast: 20 July
Patron of pregnancy, childbirth
Cause: infertility
Shrine: a miraculous well at Binsey, Oxford
   (*see* **St Frideswide**)
Symbols in art: pearl, dragon

Margaret of Scotland

Queen
1045–93. Canonised 1250

Of royal blood, Margaret was brought up in Hungary and then at **St Edward the Confessor**'s court in London. She fled after the victory of William the Conqueror. Malcolm III of Scotland gave her refuge and then married her in 1070. She was an intelligent queen who championed the adoption of Anglo-Norman customs in Scotland. Religious reformer, benefactor of the poor and foundress of Dunfermline Abbey, she was genuinely pious. Her son was King David and her daughter, Matilda, married Henry I of England.

Feast: 16 November
Patron of Scotland
Shrine: Dunfermline Abbey, Scotland

*An illuminated manuscript of St Mark with his symbol,
a winged lion, from the British Library collection*

Maria Goretti

Virgin and Martyr
1890–1902. Canonised 1950

For obvious reasons child saints are rare, but Maria Goretti's example of Christian purity and courage beyond her years was compelling enough for Pope Pius XII to canonise her in the Holy Year, 1950. The Goretti family were peasants living near Anzio in Italy and Maria, a cheerfully religious girl, suffered from the sexual attentions of a neighbour's son. When the boy eventually tried to rape her at knifepoint, she resisted and was stabbed to death. The murderer later had a vision of his victim while in jail, became a reformed character and, released after serving 27 years, was present at her canonisation. She became a popular choice as patron of new churches built in the 1950s.

Feast: 6 July
Patron of rape victims
Cause: the abolition of capital punishment

Mark the Evangelist

Apostle
d. *c*.74

Mark may be the young man in his own gospel who, collared by the mob in Gethsemane, slipped out of his tunic and escaped naked (Mark 14: 51). Acts mentions a John Mark whose family home in Jerusalem was used by the Apostles, and a Mark travelled with his cousin **St Barnabas** and **St Paul** on their first mission. He evidently angered Paul by returning prematurely to Jerusalem. Barnabas then left Paul and took Mark with him. Later Mark was with **St Peter** in Rome and seems to have made up with Paul. His gospel, perhaps written between 60 and 70, apparently gives Peter's viewpoint. Tradition says Mark died as Bishop of Alexandria, from where his relics were stolen by Venetian adventurers in 829. Hidden under a consignment of pickled pork, they were smuggled in triumph to the city-state of Venice.

Feast: 25 April
Patron of Venice
Shrine: St Mark's, Venice
Symbols in art: winged lion, writing equipment
Writings: Gospel of Mark

Martha of Bethany

Disciple of Christ
1st century

An important figure in Christ's social circle, Martha often gave him hospitality, with her sister **Mary** – possibly the Magdalene – at Bethany, taking the lead in cooking and housework while Mary talked with the Lord. It was Martha who first asked Jesus to raise their brother Lazarus from the dead and she to whom he later claimed to be 'the resurrection and the life'. In legend the three siblings later converted Provence, where Martha slew a river-dragon.

Feast: 29 July
Patron of cooks
Shrines: Aix and Tarascon, Provence
Symbols in art: dragon, cooking pot, bunch of keys

Martin de Porres

Dominican Friar
1579–1639. Canonised 1962

Martin lived all his life in Lima, Peru. The illegitimate son of a Spanish hidalgo and a native Indian woman, at 15 he joined the Rosary friary as a lay brother and eventually took charge of poor relief, the care of the sick and work amongst slaves newly shipped to Peru from Africa. He also had great devotion to all animals. A friend of **St Rose of Lima**, he was said to have powers of levitation and bilocation and despite his lowly status – he was never ordained – was consulted by many influential people on spiritual as well as worldly matters.

Feast: 3 November
Patron of hairdressers
Cause: interracial injustice
Shrine: Lima

Martin of Tours

Soldier and Bishop
315–97

Born in Hungary and educated at Pavia, Martin
was a Roman officer. Once at Amiens, moved by
the sight of a beggar at the city gates, he cut his cloak to give
the other man half. That night Christ appeared to him
wearing the divided garment and he at once became a
Christian, quit the army and took up missionary work, in
which he was active against the Arian and Priscillianist
heresies and in founding monasteries. In 371 he was named
Bishop of Tours. He combined a monk's spirituality with a
vigorous and demanding public life and was one of the
most popular saints of the Middle Ages. In France his feast
day is associated with celebrations for the autumn equinox.

Feast: 11 November
Patron of France, soldiers, drapers, furriers, tailors, geese
Causes: the French monarchy, viniculture
Shrine: Tours, France
Symbols in art: cloak, ass, globe of fire, goose

Mary (The Blessed Virgin, the Madonna)

Mother of Christ
1st century

Christ's mother is by far the pre-eminent saint of Roman and Orthodox Christendom, the object of more devotion and artistic expression than all the rest combined. Little is known of her historically, apart from a few significant mentions in the gospels. Already betrothed to **Joseph**, she accepts the Archangel Gabriel's awesome news of her pregnancy with the simple words, 'Behold, the handmaid of the Lord'. Later we glimpse her at the marriage in Cana, on Calvary and with the Apostles at Pentecost. It is an article of faith among Catholics that she was born without original sin (the Immaculate Conception) and that she was taken directly to heaven without dying (the Assumption). The latter may have taken place either in Jerusalem or in Ephesus. She is the essential intercessor for all causes. Among the metaphors used in her litany, she is star of the morning, mystical rose, tower of ivory, Ark of the Covenant and gate of heaven.

Madonna and Child with Pear *by Giovanni Bellini*
(c.1430–1516) in the Carrara Academy, Bergamo (Dagli Orti)

Feasts: 8 September (Birth of the Virgin); 15 September
(Our Lady of Sorrows); 7 October (Our Lady of the
Rosary); 8 December (Immaculate Conception);
2 January (Purification/ Presentation of the
Virgin/Candlemas); 31 May (Visitation); 15 August
(Assumption/Dormition); others

Patron of the human race in general

Shrines: Ephesus, Turkey; Lourdes, France; La Salette,
France; Fatima, Portugal; Mejudjorje, Bosnia; Knock,
Ireland

Symbols in art: wearing blue robe and veil, nursing or
holding the infant Christ in her arms

Mary Magdalene

Disciple of Jesus
1st century

In addition to the Virgin, the gospels have
several Marys whom Church tradition has
variously and confusingly combined. Mary of
Bethany (*see* **Martha**) and the unnamed female sinner who
anoints Christ's feet have, in the Western (but not the
Eastern) Church, been generally conflated with the Mary of
Magdala mentioned in the gospels as having had seven
devils cast out of her by Jesus. This tradition holds that Mary
was a repentant harlot who followed Jesus and enjoyed his
friendship. Present at Calvary, she was also (according to

Mary Magdalene by José de Ribera (1591–1652) (Dagli Orti)

St John) the first witness to the Resurrection. In tradition she later found her way to Provence, where she led a life of ascetic penitence. She is the first of several harlot saints in the canon, including Pelagia (*see* **Margaret of Antioch**) and Mary of Egypt (4th century). A 'Magdalen' is a hospital for the reform of prostitutes.

Feast: 22 July
Patron of fallen women
Shrines: St Maximin's Church and St-Baume, Aix-en-Provence; Church of Vézelay Abbey, France; La Madeleine, Paris
Symbols in art: long tangled red hair, ointments, crucifix, skull, whip

Matthew the Evangelist (Matthew the Levite)

Apostle
1st century

The credited author of the first gospel lived at Capernaum in Galilee and was a licensed tax gatherer – a despised position that nevertheless receives significant endorsement in Matthew's gospel, where Jesus twice recommends the prompt payment of taxes. Matthew was in his office when Jesus passed by with a gaggle of followers and invited him to join them. Unlike **St Peter** and

St Matthew by Michelangelo Merisi da Caravaggio (1571–1610) (Dagli Orti)

the fishermen-Apostles, he was literate and wrote his gospel originally in Hebrew or, perhaps, Aramaic – it certainly seems the work of a Palestinian Jew for other Jews. Nothing else is known about Matthew, though his martyrdom by decapitation has been placed variously in Ethiopia and Persia. His head allegedly found its way to the westernmost tip of mainland France, where his abbey's ruins still stand.

Feast: 21 September
Patron of accountants, excise officers
Shrine: Pointe de St-Mathieu, Brittany
Symbols in art: man with wings, book or scroll, sword
Writings: Gospel of St Matthew

Maximilian Kolbe

Martyr
1894–1941. Canonised 1982

Maximilian was a Pole, born at Zdunska Wola. At 16 he became a Franciscan friar and was ordained nine years later. Despite suffering from tuberculosis, he ran a Christian magazine and founded a friary in Japan. Recalled to Poland, he was superior of the 700-strong friary at Niepokalanow when the Nazis invaded. He dispersed his community but stayed to look after refugees. Kolbe's anti-Nazism led to his incarceration at Auschwitz in 1941, where he continued to work as a priest. He volunteered to replace a man whom the

SS had selected to die by starvation but survived too long (14 days) and was executed by lethal injection. The man he had replaced was present at his canonisation.

Feast: 14 August
Patron of prisoners of conscience

Michael

Archangel

The premier angel, who led the heavenly host against the insurgent Lucifer, is also close to God on Judgement Day, escorting souls and weighing them in his scales. From the 5th to the 10th centuries his cult grew in the West, where churches and shrines – most famously Mont-St-Michel in Normandy – were built on hills. In the Counter-Reformation he was invoked against Luther and Calvin. His feast is kept with the other Archangel saints, Gabriel and Raphael.

Feast: 29 September
Patron of knights, military trades, weights and measures
Causes: the defence of the Church; with Gabriel, doorkeeper of churches against the entry of devils
Shrines: Monte Gargano, Italy; Mont-St-Michel, Normandy; the Stranberg near Stuttgart; St Michael's Mount, Cornwall
Symbols in art: wings, armour, scales

Michael the Archangel by Judson Huss (Dagli Orti)

Moses the Black

Ascetic
330–405

An Ethiopian of violent manners and great strength, Moses was dismissed from the service of his Egyptian master for dishonesty and took up the life of a brigand, terrorising travellers for miles around. After a sudden conversion he joined a desert monastery in Lower Egypt, where he eventually became the abbot, known both for his piety and for his humility. When he and his brothers were attacked by Berber marauders, he refused to fight back and they were slaughtered.

Feast: 28 August
Shrine: Monastery of Dair al-Baramus, Wadi Natrun, Lower Egypt

Mungo (Kentigern)

Bishop
518–603

Mungo's royal mother, illicitly pregnant, was thrown from a cliff, then cast adrift in a coracle, finally giving birth on a lonely shore with help from the hermit St Serf, who named the child Mungo, 'dear one'. His illegitimacy was no bar to Church preferment and as Bishop of Strathclyde Mungo is later credited with establishing the Glaswegian Church. The friend of both **St Columba** and **St David**, he also travelled in Cumbria, where to his disgust he found a pagan renewal in the wake of the retreating Romans, and in west Wales, where he built a monastery at Llanelwy. Back in Glasgow, Mungo used divination in the struggle against paganism, correctly predicting that the Queen of Glasgow's lost wedding ring would be found in the belly of a salmon from the River Clyde. The fish is on Glasgow's coat of arms.

Feast: 14 January
Patron of Glasgow
Shrine: Glasgow Cathedral
Symbols in art: ring and fish

Nicholas of Myra

Bishop
c.270–350

Few facts are known about this Asia Minor bishop, but legends about him are legion. From a wealthy family, at one day old he stood up in his bath and praised God. He did many things in threes: saving three innocent men from execution, reviving three murdered

A 16th-century representation of St Nicholas of Myra in the Recklinghausen Museum

children, and rescuing a trio of poor sisters from prostitution by throwing three bags of dowry gold into their house – the origin of Christmas gifts. In 1087 his relics were brought through a storm from Myra to Bari in Apulia, ultimately becoming one of the biggest pilgrim attractions in Europe. In the north, Nicholas became merged with the pagan god Thor, of the yule log and the reindeer-drawn chariot, and so eventually (at first in America) 'Santa Claus' was born. His cult in the East is equally strong, though unconnected with Christmas.

Feast: 6 December
Patron of Russia, the Netherlands, Greece, Sicily, Apulia, merchants, sailors, pawnbrokers, children, brides, perfumiers, apothecaries
Causes: trade, sea voyages, gifts
Shrine: Bari
Symbols in art: mitre, crozier, three moneybags, anchor

Nicholas Owen

Martyr
d. 1606. Canonised 1970

The son of a carpenter at Oxford, and a man of small and twisted stature, Nicholas was from a deeply Catholic family. As the Elizabethan persecution of recusants gathered pace, he became a Jesuit lay brother whose vocation was to build hiding places for missionary priests, such as **Edmund Campion**. His brilliantly successful work – some of it undiscovered for centuries – can be seen in many country houses. His second arrest was in 1606 after the Gunpowder Plot, when he was grotesquely tortured in an attempt to obtain the location of his priest holes. He died from this treatment, having revealed no secrets, and is one of the '40 martyrs of England and Wales', a man of extraordinary, quiet courage.

Feast: 22 March
Patron of builders

Olaf of Norway (Olaf the Fat)

King
995–1030

Basically a Viking marauder, Olaf fought in England against the Danes. Returning home, he subdued the country and in 1016 became king, converting to Christianity. His harsh imposition of the new religion was unpopular and he was driven out in 1029, returning three years later only to be killed at the Battle of Stiklestad. As Christianity took hold, miracles were reported and his tomb became a great Scandinavian pilgrimage centre.

Feast: 29 July
Patron of Norway
Cause: Norwegian independence
Shrine: Cathedral of Trondheim, Norway

Oliver Plunkett

Bishop and Martyr
1625–81. Canonised 1975

An Irishman, Oliver was a priest and professor of theology in Rome for 15 years. Then, after the fall of his namesake Cromwell, he returned to Ireland to be a very able primate. But a new bout of persecution forced him underground in 1673. Six years later he was captured and brought to London, where he was convicted on false charges of treason and hanged, drawn and quartered at Tyburn.

Feast: 1 July
Shrines: Drogheda, Ireland; Downside Abbey, Somerset

Pancras

Martyr
d. 304

Pancras was a Syrian Christian, brought to Rome as a child after his parents' death, and beheaded at only 14 during the persecution by Diocletian. He was buried at Calepodius, where Rome's St Pancras church later stood, the centre of an important cult. On one occasion a perjuror swore on his tomb and had his arm paralysed, so that oaths sworn in St Pancras's name are taken to be especially binding. He is connected with railways only by the famous station sited in his London parish.

> **Feast**: 12 May
> **Patron of** railways
> **Causes**: cramp, the swearing of oaths

Patrick

Bishop and Missionary
385–461

Born in west Wales or Scotland, Patrick was the son of a deacon and grandson of a priest. At 16 he was abducted by coastal raiders to (largely) pagan Ireland. Escaping this slavery after six years, he studied for the priesthood at Auxerre, Gaul, and returned – conventionally about 432 – to convert the Irish. Legends about him abound – that he cast out the snakes, confronted the High King at Tara, lit paschal fire on the Hill of Slane – but his actual achievement was remarkable enough. The Irish were instantly attracted by his account of the new

religion and, by the end of Patrick's long tenure as Bishop at
Armagh, Christianity had been established across the land.
It quickly developed more learning and deeper sanctity than
almost anywhere in Christendom.

Feast: 17 March
Patron of Ireland and the Irish
Cause: the fear of snakes
Shrine: Croagh Patrick, County Mayo
Symbols in art: shamrock, crozier
Writings: *The Confession of St Patrick*, 'Letter to the
Soldiers of Coroticus'

Paul (Saul of Tarsus)

Apostle and Martyr
10–64

A Jew of the tribe of Benjamin and, through his
father, a Roman citizen, Saul was a tentmaker by
trade and born in the sophisticated, cosmopolitan city of
Tarsus in Asia Minor. He went in his 20s to study rabbinical
law in Jerusalem. Though small, bald and ill-favoured, he
had a fanatical personality which, by AD 35 (when he saw **St
Stephen** stoned to death), led him to become a persecutor of
Christians. He campaigned hard against the fledgling
Church until, on the Damascus road, he had an intense

vision of Christ, whom he never met in the flesh, which turned him about-face. He devoted the rest of his life to defining the central tenets of the new religion and spreading it among gentiles. After 30 years of tireless travelling and writing, he was finally put to death by beheading in Rome, it is said after converting one of Nero's favourite concubines, and traditionally on the same day as **Peter**. He is supposed to have bled milk and his head to have bounced three times, causing three springs of water to appear. His lucid and compelling epistles are the earliest Christian documents, predating the gospels. One of his many shipwrecks was on Malta, where he survived a viper's bite.

Feast: 29 June
Patron of preachers, tentmakers
Cause: snakebite
Shrines: Abbazia delle Tre Fontane and Basilica of St Paul Without-the-Walls, Rome
Symbols in art: sword, open book
Writings: Epistles of Paul

Peter (Simon Peter)

Apostle and Martyr
d. 64

Previously a married Galilean fisherman from Bethesda and part-time follower of **John the**

Baptist, Simon was the earliest Apostle to be called to be a 'fisher of men'. His pre-eminence as the first Pope derived from Jesus, who renamed him Cephas (Peter), or the rock, with the words, 'Thou art Peter, and upon this rock I will build my church and the gates of Hades shall not prevail against it. I will give unto thee the keys of the kingdom of Heaven.' He was an impetuous, illiterate man who proved all too human, three times denying his friendship with Jesus during his trial. A key figure in Acts, Peter led the Jerusalem Church, and was imprisoned by Herod Antipas (and released from his chains by an angel) before leaving for Rome, where he founded the first Christian community. Nero had him crucified – upside-down, at Peter's own request.

Feast: 29 June
Patron of the Papacy and the Apostolic Church
Cause: long life
Shrine: Basilica of St Peter, Rome
Symbols in art: keys, chains, cockerel, papal tiara
Writings: Epistle of Peter

Philip

Apostle and Martyr
1st century

Called early to the apostolate after following
John the Baptist, the Galilean Philip's

*St Philip, painted by José de Ribera between 1630 and 1639,
in the Museo del Prado, Madrid (Joseph Martin)*

appearances in the gospels are few – the best known on a mountainside in Tiberias when Jesus asked him to buy bread for the crowd that had come to hear a sermon. Philip replied there was not enough money, so Jesus worked the miracle of the loaves and the fishes – an incident suggesting Philip may have been the Apostles' quartermaster. Very few legends are told of his later life, but according to one he defeated a dragon which killed with its deadly breath. Philip is reputed to have been crucified at the age of 87 at Hierapolis, Asia Minor, when living in retirement.

Feast: 3 May
Patron of hatters, basket-weavers, pastrycooks
Cause: halitosis
Symbols in art: cross, bread basket

Philomena

Virgin and Martyr
Canonised 1837. Cult suppressed 1961

For a saint of the early Church, Philomena's cult began remarkably late. In 1802 the bones of an adolescent girl were uncovered in the Roman catacombs, near an inscription reading 'Peace be with you, Philomena'. The relics were enshrined at the church of Mugnano del Cardinale, near Nola, where miracles were soon reported. Although devotion to her grew rapidly across Catholic Europe, later archaeology has cast doubt even over the existence of the girl and she was expunged from the canon in 1961.

Feast: 11 August (5 July)
Shrine: Mugnano del Cardinale, Italy, now dismantled

Pius X (Giuseppe Sarto)

Pope
1835–1914. Canonised 1954

Born poor, the son of a sometime cobbler, postman, debt collector and repossession officer, young Giuseppe early realised his ambition to be a priest and rose steadily up the hierarchy to be Bishop of Mantua (1884) and Cardinal-Patriarch of Venice (1893). He was then a compromise choice for Pope in 1903, a pontificate marked by ferocious attacks on the 'heresy of modernism', a term which embraced materialism, egalitarian politics and all forms of ecumenism. Pius himself was an anti-intellectual of formidable physical presence. He encouraged the idea that he possessed the powers of a healer, and miracle-cures by him were reported both before and after his death.

Feast: 21 August
Causes: against communism, socialism

A portrait of Pope Pius X painted in 1903 (Dagli Orti)

Polycarp

Bishop and Martyr
69–155

Having known **John the Evangelist**, and living himself to a great age, Polycarp was a direct link between the friends of Jesus and the mid-2nd century. For 50 years he was Bishop of Smyrna, where he became known for his pacific stance, whether towards the Roman authorities or the internal wrangling of fellow Christians, saying he would rather stop his ears against heresy than argue against it. Arrested during a flare-up of anti-Christian persecution, he refused the order to curse Jesus, whom, he said, he had 'served for 83 years and he has done me no wrong'. After the failure of a move to feed him to the lions, he was stabbed to death.

Feast: 23 February
Cause: earache

Rita of Cascia

Religious
1381–1457. Canonised 1900

Rita was born near Spoleto, Italy, and wanted to be a nun, but was married at twelve to a drunkard who beat her. After 18 years her husband was killed in a pub brawl and Rita applied to join the Augustinians at Cascia, but was refused because she was not a virgin. She persisted and, in 1413, was grudgingly admitted, soon becoming known for her austere devotions. Rita developed a forehead wound which suppurated for years, stinking so badly that her sisters shunned her, but she bore her suffering with patience until her death aged 76. Today tens of thousands of pilgrims annually view her uncorrupted body in a glass coffin in Cascia, many of them victims of marital abuse.

Feast: 22 May
Patron of unhappy wives
Causes: hopelessness, despair
Shrine: Cascia, Umbria
Symbols in art: discipline, wounded forehead

Robert Southwell

Missionary, Martyr and Poet
1561–95, Canonised 1970

A Norfolk man and son of an Elizabethan courtier, Southwell was sent abroad to receive a Catholic education. He became a Jesuit and was posted as a missionary to England in 1586, where he was chaplain to the recusant Countess of Arundel until betrayed and arrested in 1592. For three years he was held in prison and repeatedly tortured, while writing intense devotional verse of the highest quality. He was hanged, drawn and quartered at Tyburn on 21 February. One of his most substantial poems is an account of Christ's passion seen through the eyes of **St Peter**.

Feast: 21 February
Shrine: Tyburn Convent, Marble Arch, London
Writings: *St Peter's Complaint*, many lyrical poems

Roch

Healer
1378–1414

A native of Montpellier, Roch is better known to legend than to history. He devoted himself early to the pilgrim's life, travelling through Italy and halting outbreaks of plague at Acquapendente, Rome and Piacenza, though in the latter place he caught the disease himself and retired to a hermitage, where a dog brought him food until he recovered. He was later arrested as a spy in Lombardy and died after a long imprisonment.

Feast: 16 August
Patron of secret agents
Cause: epidemics of bubonic plague
Symbols in art: pilgrim's garb, pointing to a plague-spot on thigh, dog carrying loaf

Rosalia

Virgin
d. *c.*1160

Rosalia came from a rich family but renounced
the world, living and dying in a hermit's cave on
Mount Pellegrino in Sicily. Bones thought to be hers (but
later said to be those of a goat) were found during the great
pestilence of 1624 and brought to Palermo, where as a saint-
protector of the city she was invoked against the epidemic.
The coincidence of her name with that of the Rosary
prompted the Jesuits to take up her cult and she became
venerated in the Spanish Netherlands in the 17th century.

Feast: 4 September
Patron of Palermo
Causes: plague, the rosary
Symbols in art: hermit's garb, garland of roses

Rose of Lima
(Isabel de Flores y del Oliva)

Ascetic and Virgin
1586–1617. Canonised 1671

The daughter of decayed Spanish gentlefolk in Peru, Rose
refused to marry and lived as a Dominican tertiary in a shed

*St Sebastian painted by Bartolommeo Vivarini (c.1432–1499),
in the collection of the Carrara Academy, Bergamo (Dagli Orti)*

in her parents' garden, where she grew flowers for sale and wore a crown of thorns and inflicted other harsh penances on herself. Her way of life was sharply criticised by her family and friends but she persisted, becoming more widely known for her visions and care for the poor. She was the first American saint and a friend of **Martin de Porres**.

Feast: 23 August
Patron of South and Central America, Peru, the Philippines, India, gardeners
Cause: the social services
Shrine: Lima
Symbols in art: roses, the Holy Child

Sebastian

Soldier and Martyr
288–318

A legendary figure, Sebastian was an officer in the pagan Emperor Domitian's Praetorian Guard and a secret Christian. When two co-religionists in the Guard were revealed, Sebastian made his own faith public and was condemned to be shot by troops from his platoon. But a member of his Christian group found him still breathing and nursed him back to health. He now boldly presented himself once more for duty, whereupon the emperor ordered him to be clubbed to death. He is a major preoccupation of art,

particularly as a focus for paintings of the male nude.
Because the Roman world connected illness with the arrows
of the god Apollo, arrows in the Christian era became
symbols of plague, a disease of violent skin eruptions.
Sebastian's recovery from his shooting made him an ideal
protector against it

Feast: 20 January
Patron of archers, athletes, soldiers
Cause: epidemics (especially bubonic plague)
Symbol in art: arrows piercing his flesh

Simeon Stylites (Simeon of the Pillar)

Ascetic
390–459

Simeon, a native of Cilicia, close to the Syrian
border, was a monk of such asceticism that he was
ejected from his community. Thereafter he was a hermit, but
when crowds sought him out from sheer curiosity, he built
himself a succession of pillars, the tallest 60 ft (18 m) high and
6 ft (1.8m) in diameter, on which he lived, never coming
down. Clothed in festering animal skins, placing maggots to
feast on his flesh and fasting continually, he depended entirely
on others for food and water. Meanwhile he preached daily

against lust and luxury and was consulted by the highest in the land. A 500-year tradition of desert pillar-saints followed. Simeon is the subject of a poem by Tennyson. His pillar's base can still be seen at Qala'at Samaan.

Feast: 5 January
Shrines: Qala'at Samaan; Antioch
Symbol in art: pillar

Simon the Zealot (The Canaanite)

Apostle and Martyr
1st century

The gospels give us no details of Simon apart from listing him as an Apostle and identifying him with the town of Cana and the political Zealot movement, guerrilla fighters led by the fiery Judas of Gamala against the Roman occupation of Judaea. He must have left the Zealots, since Christ's pacifism was incompatible with their methods. Simon's former political affiliations are played down by artists. His status as brother of **St Jude** and **St James the Less** is stressed instead, and he is sometimes confused with them. The manner of his martyrdom is particular to him: his head was sawn off while he was still alive.

Feast: 28 October (with St Jude)
Symbols in art: saw, fish, oar, axe

Stephen

Martyr
d. 35

In Acts, seven deacons are appointed to assist the Apostles in alms-giving, one of whom was the Greek-speaking Stephen. When his eloquent preaching came to the notice of the Sanhedrin, he was summoned for blasphemy and made a fiery defence speech ('you stiff-necked and uncircumcised hearts and ears'). Outraged, they condemned him to be stoned to death, at which the still anti-Christian Saul of Tarsus – later **St Paul** – was present as an observer. The first after Jesus to die for the faith, Stephen is revered by some as the 'protomartyr'.

Feast: 26 December
Patron of deacons
Cause: headaches
Shrine: his relics were taken to Constantinople and later Rome
Symbols in art: deacon's dalmatic, stones, palm

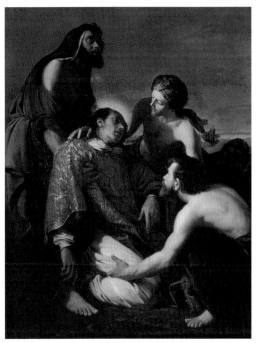

The Recovery of the Body of St Stephen *(1853)*
by Bernardo Celentano (Dagli Orti)

Swithin

Bishop
d. 862

As adviser of kings Egbert and Ethewulf of Wessex, Swithin was an influential figure. He is said to have disliked pomp and diverted funds into church building and keeping diocesan records – a vital source for later historians. Miracles performed by Swithin included mending a batch of broken eggs when a poor woman's market stall was pushed over by a hooligan. The belief that the weather conditions on his feast day will determine those of the next 40 days comes from the 40 days of rain which delayed the dedication of a new shrine to him in Winchester Cathedral in 971.

Feast: 2 July (formerly 15 July)
Cause: drought
Shrine: Winchester Cathedral

Teresa of Avila
(Teresa de Cepeda y Ahumada)

Mystic, Foundress and Doctor of the Church
1515–82. Canonised 1622. Doctor 1970

Teresa is one of the most complex and fascinating of saints. Born at Avila in Castile, she became a Carmelite and, despite

*St Teresa of Avila by Fray Juan de la Miseria in the
St Teresa Convent, Avila (Joseph Martin)*

early setbacks and attacks of painful illness, her devotions
yielded some of the most graphic mystical experiences ever
known to the Church. She was also a reformer and an
ecclesiastical politician who was against what she saw as the
laxity of the Order. In 1562, opposed by many, she founded
the St Joseph Convent for strictly enclosed nuns. Other
foundations followed. She travelled across Spain, battling
against the unreformed (calced) Carmelites until the
reformed (uncalced or barefoot) Order, which she had
instigated with her friend and ally **St John of the Cross**, was
recognised by the hierarchy. Her books and letters form an
unsurpassed body of spiritual and mystical literature.

Feast: 15 October
Patron of Carmelite Order
Symbols in art: Carmelite habit, angel with spear or dart
Writings: *Autobiography of St Teresa, The Way of
Perfection, The Interior Castle*

Teresa of Lisieux
(Thérèse Martin)

Religious and Doctor of the Church
1873–97. Canonised 1925. Doctor of the Church 1997

As a Carmelite nun in her Normandy home town, Teresa
lived an obscure life, and despite her reputation for

sweetness and simple holiness, she hardly stood out from the other sisters. But she had been asked by her spiritual director to write down her childhood memories, which she called *The Story of a Soul*. Published after her painful death from tuberculosis at only 24, it struck a tremendous chord and became a worldwide best-seller. Examples of her miraculous intercession flooded in and canonisation became irresistible. Today a visit to her vast basilica-shrine is one of the world's most popular pilgrimages and in 1997 Pope John Paul II declared her only the third female Doctor of the Church.

Feast: 3 October
Patron of France, Australia, Carmelite novices, florists, flower growers
Cause: missions
Shrine: Lisieux, Normandy
Symbol in art: bouquet of roses
Writings: *The Story of a Soul*

Theodore of Canterbury

Bishop
602–90

In 667 Theodore was a 66-year-old Greek monk from Tarsus when Pope St Vitalian asked him to fill the vacant see of

Canterbury. Theodore proved a great organiser, and with his energy and leadership the English Church was overhauled, making it a mature, disciplined body. His tenure involved controversy, such as the row with **St Wilfrid** of York, but the framework he created was so enduring it still exists today. When, after 22 years in office, he died at Canterbury he was venerated for his wisdom and learning.

Feast: 19 September
Shrine: Canterbury
Source: Bede's *History of England*

Thomas à Becket

Bishop and Martyr
1118–70. Canonised 1173

Becket was a charismatic figure who revelled in adulation. As friend and Chancellor of **Henry II** of England, he fully backed the king's attempts to reassert his control over Church affairs. But when Henry made him Archbishop of Canterbury in 1162, Becket changed. Abandoning worldliness for a new asceticism, he did all he could to thwart the king and as a result was assassinated in his cathedral by four knights who thought (not quite correctly) they were doing Henry's will. The king did public penance and within three years Becket was canonised, quickly becoming the most revered saint in England, a potent

The murder of Thomas à Becket, from a 13th-century manuscript

symbol of the rights of Church over state and a martyr with a phenomenally popular shrine. Henry VIII, for his own obvious reasons, had this obliterated.

Feast: 29 December
Shrine: Canterbury
Symbols in art: pallium, mitre and archbishop's cross, sword penetrating his skull

---

Thomas Aquinas

Doctor of the Church
1225–74. Canonised 1323. Doctor 1567

Thomas was born in Calabria, to a noble family. After a Benedictine education he joined the Dominicans against his family's wishes and – although at first concealing his learning so successfully he was known as 'the dumb ox' – he proceeded to distinguish himself in theology, primarily at the University of Paris. Aquinas was vast in both physical bulk and intellect, but there was a quality of humility and sweetness about him which earned him a second nickname, 'Angelic Doctor'. His analysis of the competing but (he argued) compatible claims of faith and reason, and its reconciliation of pagan philosophy with Christianity, left an indelible impression on philosophy and theology.

Feast: 28 January
Symbols in art: star on breast, ox, book, lily
Writings: *Summa Contra Gentiles, Summa Theologica*

Thomas Didymus

Apostle and Martyr
1st century

Thomas's surname means 'the twin', but nothing is recorded about his sibling. He is the 'doubting Thomas' who, absent when Christ reappeared among the Apostles, refused at first to believe it. This scene was apocryphally reprised when he later disbelieved the Virgin's assumption. Thomas in legend refused to go on a mission to India, whereupon Christ appeared and sold him in slavery to an Indian prince. He may have founded an isolated wing of the Church, discovered by Vasco da Gama on his arrival in India in 1498. Thomas is said to have been at cross-purposes with one Indian ruler when, having promised to build him a palace, he revealed he was referring to a dwelling in Paradise. His feast day was traditionally one on which employers bought seasonal drinks for their staff, known as 'Thomasing'.

Feast: 21 December
Patron of builders and architects
Symbols in art: set-square, belt, spear, dagger

Thomas More

Martyr
1478–1535. Canonised 1935

More was a Renaissance man in both a literal and a broader sense. He had a reputation as the most brilliant English humanist of his time but he was also a man of great versatility, rising to the top in law, politics, academia and literature, as well as being a patron of the arts, educator, loving family man and devout Catholic. But his worldly career was cut short when Henry VIII, in an episode reminiscent of Henry II's clash with **Thomas à Becket**, took over the Church in order to divorce his queen and More could not support him. More was incarcerated, tried for treason, convicted and beheaded on Tower Hill, just days after his friend Bishop **John Fisher**, with whom he shares a feast day. In prison he wrote works of great spirituality. Pope John Paul II declared him patron of politicians.

> **Feast:** 22 June
> **Patron of** lawyers, politicians
> **Writings:** *Utopia, Dialogue of Comfort Against Tribulation, Treatise on the Passion of Christ*

St Ursula and the King (1490–98), *painted by Vittore Carpaccio (c.1450–1525/6) and held in the collection of the Accademia, Venice*

Ursula

Virgin and Martyr
3rd–4th century. Cult suppressed 1969

One of the most popular saints of the Middle Ages and the subject of a great cycle of paintings by Carpaccio, Ursula is almost entirely the product of legend. Said to be a British princess, she avoided marriage to a pagan chieftain by making a pilgrimage to Rome with a vast retinue of 11,000 virgins. On the way back they were all massacred by Hun tribesmen at Cologne after Ursula refused to yield to the advances of the Huns' leader.

> **Feast:** 21 October
> **Patron of** Cologne, Venice
> **Cause:** the education of girls
> **Shrine:** Cologne
> **Symbols in art:** arrow, clock, ship

Valentine

Martyr
3rd century

Like **St Nicholas**, Valentine's cult is widespread but known details of his life are few. Apparently two Valentines have been conflated: a priest, martyred in Rome in the 3rd century, and a bishop of Terni, Umbria, also martyred in Rome. His patronage of lovers, and the sending of cards on his feast day, may derive from the belief that birds look for mates in mid-February.

Feast: 14 February
Patron of lovers
Cause: erotic and romantic love
Shrines: Carmelite Church, Dublin; The Gorbals Franciscan Pastoral Centre, Glasgow
Symbols in art: rose bush, birds, heart pierced by arrow

Vincent de Paul

Missionary
1581–1660. Canonised 1737

From a poor peasant family in Gascony, Vincent was ordained priest at only 20 and quickly proved himself a rising star in the Church. Royalty and nobility alike admired his sensitivity and principles. But rivals falsely accused him of theft and, since he refused to defend himself, it took six months for the charges to be disproved. He then dedicated himself to diverting funds from the rich to the poor. He founded several Orders for charitable work, one with a widowed aristocrat. He was influenced by **St Francis of Sales** and worked among street children and galley slaves.

> **Feast:** 27 September
> **Patron of** charities
> **Cause:** alleviation of poverty and suffering

Vitus

Martyr
*c.*300. Cult suppressed 1969

Solid evidence about Vitus is almost non-existent but he was probably Sicilian. In legend he was a child of cruel parents, and escaped to Italy with his nurse and his tutor. Vitus made an early success by exorcising a demon from the emperor's son. But he and his companions were persecuted and then martyred. His association with nervous diseases presumably comes from successful cures at his tomb.

> **Feast:** 15 June
> **Patron** of dancers, actors, sufferers from nervous diseases
> **Causes:** epilepsy, rabid dogbites, snakebites, storms

Wenceslas (Vaclav, Wenzel)

Prince and Martyr
907–29. Cult dating from 985

Wenceslas is known through the fictional story in the Victorian Christmas carol by J.M. Neale. He was not a king but the son of the Duke of Bohemia, when paganism vied for power with Christianity. Wenceslas's paternal grandmother, St Ludmila, made him a Christian but his pagan mother had her murdered and took power. When she was deposed Wenceslas, at the age of 15, was duke. He reintroduced Christianity and became a just ruler, but was killed in his brother's castle at the age of 22.

Feast: 28 September
Patron of Bohemia, Moravia, brewers
Symbols in art: banner, eagle, staff

Wilfrid

Bishop
634–709

Wilfrid was one of the earliest northern English monks to adopt the Roman style. He founded monasteries and, backed by the king of Northumbria, argued at the Synod of Whitby (664) against the Celtic-minded **St Hilda**. There he faced a rival Celtic candidate, St Chad. With **St Theodore**'s help he triumphed and built York into a power base. This led to quarrels with Theodore and the king, and Wilfrid was deposed. He went into self-imposed European exile. After a reconciliation in 705 he became Bishop of Hexham and Abbot of Ripon, where his turbulent career ended.

Feast: 12 October
Shrines: Ripon Abbey; St Andrew's, Oundle,
Northamptonshire

Willibrord

Bishop and Missionary
658–739

Although a Northumbrian, Willibrord is hardly known in his native land but is famous in continental Europe, especially in the Low Countries. Educated at Ripon Abbey, he was a protégé of **St Wilfrid**, who sent him across the North Sea with eleven companion monks to evangelise Friesland. Willibrord settled in Utrecht, where Pope Sergius I named him bishop. In 700 he founded the monastery of Echternach in Luxembourg, where he died four decades later. In a long career he enjoyed the patronage of the powerful leaders Pepin of Herstal and Charles Martel, and from 719 he was assisted by **St Boniface**, on his way to convert Germany.

Feast: 7 November
Patron of Friesland
Shrine: Echternach, Luxembourg

Winifrid (Gwenfrewi)

Virgin
d. c.650

A certain Prince Caradoc made advances to the young Winifrid and, after she repulsed him, he struck off her head in a fury. Where the head fell a miraculous spring appeared on the spot, now Holywell, by the estuary of the River Dee in North Wales. It is said that her uncle St Beuno restored her head and her life, after which she became a famous abbess at Gwytherin, Denbighshire. St Winifrid was one of three saints (with **SS George** and **David**) mentioned in a 1415 statute ordering their special veneration in England and Wales. Her well has remained a favourite place of pilgrimage, especially for sick women.

Feast: 3 November
Patron of sick or infertile women
Cause: gynaecological complaints
Shrine: Holywell, North Wales
Symbols in art: sword, head held in hands

PILGRIMAGES

A saint's shrine (see individual entries) generally means either the place of death or the resting place of the remains (in Catholic parlance, the relics). A few shrines, such as Lourdes, commemorate not a person's life and death but a miracle.

To make a pilgrimage is an adventure, and may be a trial, but it is also, as Thomas Merton wrote, a human instinct. Spiritually, some pilgrims seek redemption, a way back to a lost point of origin – health, faith, innocence. In this case it is an outward expression of an inner journey. Others wish to journey outwards to new spiritual destinations. But a pilgrimage is undertaken for more ordinary motives, too: to fulfil a promise, give thanks, remit one's sins, make an offering, gain an indulgence ior simply have a holiday. The greatest pilgrimage era was the Middle Ages when, as Chaucer's *Canterbury Tales* shows, it was almost equivalent to mass tourism.

Pilgrims today are sometimes disconcerted by the quantities of religious souvenirs on sale at sites. But this commercialism should be compared with the excesses of the past, when pilgrims were routinely stripped of everything they owned – down to their clothes – for the privilege of accessing a shrine. Pilgrimage in the Middle Ages was often a racket. Miracles and relics were manufactured, indulgences bought and sold, lodgings priced impossibly high, all in an atmosphere of hysterical credulity. Yet, in spite of everything, the pilgrims kept coming, and they still do.

The Five Great Medieval Pilgrimages

THE HOLY LAND

The foremost Christian pilgrimage has always been to Israel and Palestine. Bethlehem and Jerusalem are the major draws, but pilgrims also seek out the locations of prominent events in the New Testament, such as Nazareth, Cana, Capernaum and the Sea of Galilee. The enormous prestige of the Holy Land has been accompanied by commensurate difficulties for the pilgrim, not least that it has been and remains a place of danger and conflict. This, for many, has merely increased its attraction.

ROME

With 'all roads' leading to it, the second pilgrimage site of Christendom was always easier to reach than the Holy Land, though not necessarily safer. The primary medieval attractions, apart from the scale and splendour of Papal ceremonial, were the heads of **SS Peter** and **Paul** and the relics of **John the Evangelist** in their respective basilicas, and the head of **St Thomas** in S. Maria Maggiore. There were scores of other relics, such as a piece of **St Lawrence**'s flesh or St Veronica's veil. Roman pilgrims also visited shrines along the way. A pilgrim en route from southern France, for example, might view St Etienne at Toulouse, **St Giles** at Arles, **St Mary Magdalene** at Aix and **St Ambrose** at Milan.

SANTIAGO DE COMPOSTELA

Well-trodden routes across France and Spain led to the enormously prestigious shrine of **St James the Great** in Galicia, near the north-west tip of Iberia, the name itself a corruption of the Italian *Giacomo apostolo*. Medieval pilgrims to Santiago wore on their hats cockle- or scallop-shells to signify St James, and these were blessed by their parish priest before departure. They warded off evil during the journey and had an added use as drinking vessels.

CANTERBURY

The shrine of **Thomas à Becket** was one of the wealthiest in Europe. When Henry VIII suppressed it, he took away 27 cartloads of precious stones and metals. As at other shrines, *ex voto* offerings were made to commemorate the saint's successful intercessions. Mostly wax effigies (for example of limbs), they included some gruesome curiosities such as Henry of Maldon's tapeworm, which was hung in the cathedral for general appraisal.

COLOGNE

The cathedral was believed to possess the relics of the three Magi who presented gifts to the infant Jesus at Bethlehem. Not least because the Magi were themselves the original Christian pilgrims, Cologne Cathedral became one of the most popular and of all shrines.

Pilgrimages of Mary

The pilgrimage world today is dominated more than ever by the cult of the Virgin **Mary**. Visionary appearances by Christ's mother, often to children, have proliferated and pilgrims flock to the resulting shrines. Lourdes remains the largest of these, closely followed by Fatima (a personal favourite of Pope John Paul II, since he survived an assassination attempt on the feast of Our Lady of Fatima), but similar phenomena have been seen around the world, ranging from those attracting millions to tiny local shrines with merely a cave, a holy spring and a statue of the Virgin to show.

Some celebrated Marian shrines, with dates of the Virgin's appearances are:

Argentina: Mary of the Rosary, San Nicolas (1983)

Austria: Our Lady of the Bowed Head, Vienna (1610)

Belgium: The Virgin of the Poor, Banneux (1933)
Our Lady with the Golden Heart, Beauraing (1932)

Bosnia: The Virgin of Medjugorje (1981)

England: Our Lady of Walsingham

France: Our Lady of La Salette, French Alps (1846)
Our Lady of Lourdes, French Pyrenees
(1858, St Bernadette)
Our Lady of the Smile, Lisieux, Normandy
(1883, St Teresa)

Germany: Our Lady with the Golden Horse, Altötting,
Bavaria

Ireland: Our Lady Queen of Ireland, Knock, County
Mayo (1879)

Italy: Our Lady of Montallegro, Rapallo (1557)
The Weeping Madonna of Syracuse, Sicily (1953)

Japan: The Holy Mother of Akita (1973)

Mexico: Our Lady of the Roses, Guadalupe (1531)

Poland: The Black Madonna of Czestochowa

Portugal: Our Lady of Fatima (1916)

Rwanda: Our Lady of Kibeho (1981)

South Africa: Our Lady Tabernacle of the Most High,
Ngome, Natal (1955)

Spain: Our Lady of Mount Carmel, Garabandal, Santander (1961)

Syria: Our Lady of Damascus (1982)

USA: Our Lady of America, Fostoria, Ohio (1956)

Selected 'Minor' Medieval Pilgrimages

BARI

The bones of **St Nicholas** had been stolen from their tomb at Myra in Asia Minor in 1087 and taken to Bari, Italy, where they made the basis for a phenomenally successful pilgrimage centre.

MONT-ST-MICHEL

In the 14th century, Europe's great shrine to **St Michael** in Normandy became a major destination for pilgrim-children. The spectacularly sited monastery has remained a busy pilgrimage site, but it can be hard to distinguish devout from profane tourism.

PARIS

Apart from **St Louis IX**'s remains, the Ste-Chapelle possessed relics acquired by the saintly king himself, including a crown of thorns alleged to have been Christ's. Other important shrines included those of **St Denis** at Montmartre and **St Geneviève**.

TOURS

The tomb of **St Martin** lay in this cathedral and may have converted King Clovis to Christianity. Since this led to Christianity taking hold in France, the shrine had enormous prestige.

TRONDHEIM

Norway's national saint, **Olaf**, was buried here, making it the greatest shrine in Scandinavia.

VÉZELAY

This abbey in a Burgundian backwater became a wealthy resort of pilgrims during the 11th century when the story spread that this was **St Mary Magdalene**'s burial place. By 1146 it was so celebrated that **St Bernard** and **St Louis IX** launched the Second Crusade here and, in 1181, it was the starting point of the Third Crusade. Vézelay's decline was rapid, and by the mid-13th century the pilgrimage was less popular.

Pilgrimage in Britain and Ireland

Founded on relics, and usually in need of the revenue of pilgrim-tourists, the great cathedrals have always drawn travellers in large numbers. In addition to the one at Canterbury, important cathedral shrines include Oxford (**St Frideswide**), Chester (St Werberga), Lichfield (St Chad), Lincoln (**St Hugh**), Durham (**SS Bede** and **Cuthbert**), Ely (**St Etheldreda**), Winchester (**St Swithin**), **St David's**, Glasgow (**St Mungo**) and, in London, Westminster Abbey (the Holy Blood and **St Edward the Confessor**) and St Paul's (St Erkenwald).

Britain also abounds in holy mounts and islands, sacred woods, magic grottoes and miraculous springs. Many of these originated in Druid religion but were easily adapted to Christianity, usually by being associated with a saint. The island of Iona, the home of **St Columba**, remains popular to this day, as does **St Cuthbert**'s Lindisfarne. **St Hilda**'s Whitby, raised high above the sea, is a hilltop shrine and **St Joseph of Arimathea**'s tomb at Glastonbury has the Tor nearby. Of the hundreds of sacred springs, those of Holywell (**St Winifrid**), **St Mary**'s at Willesden and Our Lady of Walsingham have retained their illustrious reputations to the present day.

In Ireland, the most prominent of sacred islands is on Lough Derg, attracting pilgrims with a special interest in penance. Irish mountains with saintly associations are numerous, two of the most notable being Croagh Patrick and Mount Brandon (**St Brendan**). Skellig Michael off the coast of County Kerry combines features of both the island and the mountain: a stark rock 10 miles offshore and rearing 700 feet from the sea, it is among the most dramatic of all old ascetic-monastic sites. One curious pilgrimage destination is St Fintan's Tree, Clonenagh, County Laois, a sycamore standing near the site of St Fintan's 6th-century monastery. Water that collects in a slot in the tree is invested with healing powers.

Saints' Days

Saints which have sections dedicated to them within the main text are highlighted in **bold**.

January
1 Abbot Clarus
2 **Basil the Great**, Gregory of Nazianzus, **Mary**
3 **Geneviève of Paris**
4 **Elizabeth Seton**, Roger of Ellant
5 **Simeon Stylites**
6 Melanius
7 Raymond of Peñafort
8 Lucian, Nathalan
9 Adrian of Canterbury
10 Peter Orseolo
11 Alexander
12 Benedict Biscop
13 Bishop Hilary
14 Felix of Nola, **Mungo**
15 Ita
16 Bernard and his Companions
17 Antony the Abbot
18 Prisca
19 Canute IV, King of Denmark
20 Fabian, **Sebastian**
21 **Agnes**
22 Vincent of Saragossa
23 Emerentiana
24 **Francis of Sales**
25 Dwyn
26 Paula
27 Angela Merici
28 **Thomas Aquinas**
29 Gildas
30 Bathild
31 John Bosco

February
1 Brigid of Ireland
2 Joan de Lestonnac
3 **Aelred**, **Blaise**
4 John de Britto, Gilbert of Sempringham
5 **Agatha**

30 John Climacus
31 Benjamin

April
1 Hugh of Grenoble
2 Francis of Paola
3 Richard of Chichester
4 Benedict the Black, **Isidore of Seville**
5 Vincent Ferrer
6 William of Eskill
7 John Baptist de la Salle
8 Walter of Pontoise
9 Waudru
10 Michael de Sanctis
11 Stanislaus
12 Pope Martin I
13 Guinoch
14 Tiburtius and Valerian
15 Ruadhan
16 **Bernadette**, Magnus of Orkney
17 Donnan
18 Apollonius the Apologist
19 Expeditus
20 Caedwalla, King of Wessex
21 **Anselm**
22 Theodore of Sykeon
23 **George**
24 Ivo

25 **Mark the Evangelist**
26 Cletus
27 Zita
28 Peter Mary Chanel
29 **Catherine of Siena**
30 Pius V

May
1 **Joseph the Worker**, Peregrine Laziosi
2 Athanasius
3 Alexander and Eventius, **James the Less**, **Philip**
4 Florian
5 Asaph
6 Adbert
7 John of Beverley
8 Victor Maurus
9 Pachomius
10 Cathal
11 Gengulf
12 **Pancras**
13 Andrew Fournet, Caradoc
14 Apostle Matthias
15 **Dympna**, **Isidore the Ploughman**
16 **Brendan the Navigator**, Honoratus, John of Nepomuk, Ubald
17 Paschal Baylon

18 Venantius, John I

19 **Dunstan**, Ivo of Kermartin, Pope Celestine V

20 Bernardino of Siena

21 Godric

22 **Rita of Cascia**

23 William of Rochester

24 David of Scotland

25 Gregory VII, **Madeleine-Sophie Barat**

26 Philip Neri, **Augustine of Canterbury** (in England)

27 **Augustine of Canterbury**, **Bede the Venerable**

28 Bernard of Montjoux

29 Bona

30 Ferdinand III of Castile, **Joan of Arc**

31 **Mary**, Petronilla

June

1 **Gwen Teirbron**, Nicomede

2 Erasmus (Elmo)

3 Charles Lwanga, **Joseph Mkasa**

4 Petroc

5 **Boniface**

6 Norbert

7 Colman of Dromore

8 William of York

9 **Columba**

10 Landerious of Paris

11 **Barnabas**

12 Ternan

13 **Anthony of Padua**

14 Dogmael

15 **Vitus**

16 John Francis Regis

17 **Alban** (in England)

18 Mark and Marcellian

19 Romuald

20 Adalbert of Magdeburg, Mary, Our Lady of Consolation

21 Aloysius

22 **John Fisher**, **Thomas More**

23 Agrippina, **Etheldreda**

24 **John the Baptist**

25 Febronia

26 Anthelm

27 Cyril of Alexandria, Kyned

28 Austell

29 **Paul**, **Peter**

30 Erentrude

July

1 **Oliver Plunkett**, Serf

2 Otto, **Swithin**

3 Germanus of Man

4 Elizabeth of Portugal

5 Modwenna, **Philomena**

6 Maria Goretti

7 Hedda of Winchester

8 Bishop Kilian

9 Everildis, **Virgin Mary, Queen of Peace**

10 The Seven Brothers

11 Drostan

12 John Gualbert, Veronica

13 Henry II

14 Camillus de Lellis

15 Bonaventure

16 Helier

17 Kenelm

18 Edburga of Winchester

19 Gervase, Protase

20 Margaret of Antioch (Marina)

21 Laurence of Brindisi

22 Mary Magdalene

23 Apollinaris

24 Boris and Gleb, Christina

25 Christopher, **James the Great**

26 Anne

27 The Seven Sleepers of Ephesus

28 Samson

29 Martha of Bethany, Olaf of **Norway**

30 Adbon, Sennen

31 Ignatius of Loyola

August

1 Alphonsus Liguori, Faith, Hope and Charity, Nicodemus

2 Theodota of Nicaea

3 Germanus of Auxerre

4 Molua, Sithney

5 Afra

6 Sixtus

7 Pope Sixtus II

8 Cyriacus, **Dominic**, John **Baptist Vianney**

9 Emygdius

10 Lawrence

11 Clare of Assisi, Philomena

12 Attracta

13 Hippolytus, Cassian of Imola

14 Athanasia of Aegina, **Maximilian Kolbe**

15 Mary the Virgin

16 Roch, Stephen of Hungary

17 Hyacinth

18 Helena
19 John Eudes
20 **Bernard of Clairvaux**
21 Pius X
22 Symphorian
23 **Rose of Lima**
24 Bartholomew
25 **Louis IX of France**,
Genesius the Comedian
26 Ninian
27 Monica
28 **Augustine of Hippo,
Moses the Black**
29 Sebbi
30 Felix and Adauctus, **Fiacre**
31 **Aidan**, Raymond Nonnatus

September
1 **Giles**
2 Brocard
3 Bassillissa, **Gregory the
Great**
4 Macnissi, **Rosalia**
5 Lawrence Giustiniani
6 Magnus of Fussen
7 Evurtius
8 Adrian, **Mary**, Natalia
9 Ciaran of Clonmacnoise
10 Nicholas of Tolentino
11 Deiniol

12 Guy of Anderlecht
13 **John Chrysostom**, Venerius
14 Notburga
15 **Mary**, Nicomedes
16 Cornelius, Ninian
17 Lambert
18 Joseph of Cupertino
19 Januarius, **Theodore of
Canterbury**
20 Eustace
21 **Matthew the Evangelist**
22 Maurice
23 Adamnan, Eunan
24 Gerard of Csanad
25 Finbar
26 **Cosmas and Damian**,
Cyprian
27 **Vincent de Paul**
28 Bernard of Feltre,
Wenceslas
29 Gabriel the Archangel,
Michael the Archangel,
Raphael the Archangel
30 **Jerome**

October
1 Remigius
2 Leger
3 Hewald the Dark and
Hewald the Fair,

Teresa of Lisieux
4 **Francis of Assisi**
5 Maurus, Placid
6 **Bruno**, Faith (Foi)
7 **Mary**, Osith
8 **Bridget**, Pelagia
   the Penitent
9 **Denis**, Bishop of Paris,
   John Leonardi
10 Paulinus of York
11 Canice (Kenneth)
12 Ethelburga of Barking,
   Wilfrid
13 **Edward the Confessor**
14 Callistus I
15 **Teresa of Avila**
16 Hedwig
17 Ignatius of Antioch
18 **Luke the Evangelist**
19 **Frideswide**, Paul of the
   Cross
20 Maria Boscardin
21 Fintan Munnu, **Ursula**
22 Donatus of Fiesole
23 John of Capistrano
24 Antony Claret
25 **Crispin and Crispinian**,
   Margaret Clitherow,
   Marnock
26 Eata

27 Frumentius
28 **Jude, Simon the Zealot**
29 Colman of Kilmacduagh
30 Marcellus the Centurion
31 Bega (Bee)

November
1 All Saints' Day
2 Marcian (Cyrrhus)
3 Piriminus, **Martin de
   Porres**, Hubert, **Winifrid**
4 **Charles Borromeo**
5 **Elizabeth and Zachary**
6 Leonard of Noblac, Winnoc
7 **Willibrord**
8 Four Crowned Martyrs
9 Benignus (Benen)
10 Andrew Avellino, **Leo the
   Great**
11 **Martin of Tours**
12 Josaphat
13 Britius, Homobonus
14 Lawrence O'Toole
15 Albert the Great, Fintan of
   Rheinau
16 **Margaret of Scotland**
17 Gregory the Wonderworker,
   Hilda of Whitby, Hugh of
   Lincoln
18 Mawes

19 **Elizabeth of Hungary**,
   Nerses I
20 **Edmund**
21 Albert of Louvain
22 **Cecilia**
23 Clement I, Columban
24 Chrysogonus, **John of the Cross**
25 **Catherine of Alexandria**
26 John Berchmans
27 Catherine Laboure,
   Maximus
28 James of the Marches
29 Saturninus
30 **Andrew**

December
 1 **Edmund Campion**,
   Eligius (Eloi)
 2 Chromatius
 3 **Francis Xavier**
 4 **Barbara**, John Damascene
 5 Birinus, Crispina
 6 **Nicholas of Myra**
 7 **Ambrose**
 8 Budoc, **Mary**

 9 Peter Fourier
10 Eulalia
11 Damasus, Corentin,
   Gentian
12 **Finnian of Clonard**, Jeanne
   Françoise de Chantal
13 **Lucy**
14 **John of the Cross**
15 Mary di Rosa
16 Adelaide
17 Begga
18 Flannan
19 Anastasius I
20 Dominic of Silos
21 Peter Canisius,
   Thomas Didymus
22 Chaeremon
23 John of Kanty
24 Delphinus
25 Anastasia, Eugenia
26 **Stephen**
27 **John the Evangelist**
28 The Holy Innocents
29 **Thomas à Becket**
30 Egwin
31 Sylvester

GLOSSARY

Absolution: sacramental forgiveness of sins.

Albigensian: sect of 12th–13th centuries with unorthodox beliefs about good and evil.

anchorite: hermit, one who lives cut off from human contact

apostle: one of twelve chosen by Christ to follow him.

Arian: heretic with unorthodox beliefs about the nature of God and the nature of Christ; follower of Arius (4th century).

ascetic: one who chooses a life of self-denial and prayer.

Benedictine: monk of the Order founded by St Benedict.

bilocation: miraculous ability to be in two places at once.

canonisation: process whereby the Church recognises a saint.

Carmelite: friar wearing white habit, originating in the 12th century.

Carthusian: monk of the Benedictine Order of St Bruno.

charterhouse: Carthusian monastery.

Christendom: the Christian faith as a whole, including Roman Catholic, Orthodox and Protestant churches.

Cistercian: Order of monks adhering strictly to Benedictine Rule.

contemplative: religious life devoted to meditation and prayer.

dalmatic: deacon's ceremonial gown or vestment.

Doctor of the Church: writer or teacher officially recognised by the Church as having advanced theology and religious devotion.

Dominican: Order of friars founded by St Dominic.

episcopate: bishop's period of office; diocese.

Fathers of the Church: early saints who formed the spiritual practice of the early Church, e.g. SS Jerome, Augustine of

Hippo, Leo the Great.

Franciscan: friar of Order founded by St Francis.

friar: member of a mendicant (i.e. begging) religious Order.

heretic: one whose beliefs conflict with those of the Church.

indulgence: remission from punishment after death, usually earned by prayer or pilgrimage and measured in time

Jesuit: member of St Ignatius's Society of Jesus.

levitation: miraculous ability to rise above the ground.

martyr: one who gives up his or her life for a religious belief.

monophysite: heretic with unorthodox beliefs about the nature of Christ (5th century onwards).

Order: organisation of monks or nuns.

pagan: non-Christian.

pallium: white woollen ceremonial robe worn by the Pope.

Primate: the most senior bishop in a designated country.

Priscillianism: Spanish heresy of the 4th and 5th centuries, named after Bishop Priscillian of Avila, put to death for sorcery.

proselytising: converting from one faith to another.

recusant: Catholic in England who refused to acknowledge the Protestant monarch as head of the Church of England.

relic: object associated with a sacred event or saint, often a portion of the body preserved after death.

religious: member of a religious Order.

see: area under bishop's authority.

shrine: place of pilgrimage linked with a sacred event or saint.

stigmata: marks of Christ's wounds.

tertiary: lay person who takes limited vows.

veneration: paying special attention in prayer and meditation to a particular saint, often through a relic.

COLLINS GEM
1950s
a mine of information

COLLINS GEM
1960s
a mine of information

COLLINS GEM
1970s
NO GAS
a mine of information

COLLINS GEM
1980s
a mine of information

COLLINS | Jane's
CIVIL
AIRCRAFT
a mine of information

COLLINS GEM
CLANS
& Tartans

COLLINS GEM
Classic
TV SERIES
a mine of information

COLLINS | Jane's
COMBAT
AIRCRAFT
a mine of information

COLLINS GEM
FIRSTS
a mine of information

COLLINS GEM
GOLF

COLLINS GEM
HILLWALKER'S
Survival Guide
a mine of information

COLLINS GEM
HOME
EMERGENCY GUIDE
a mine of information

COLLINS GEM
Collecting
STAMPS
a mine of information

COLLINS GEM
STARS
a mine of information

COLLINS GEM
SUPERSTITIONS
a mine of information

COLLINS GEM
Using Your
SOFTWARE
a mine of information